Ubuntu Netbooks

The Path to Low-Cost Computing

Sander van Vugt

Apress®

Ubuntu Netbooks: The Path to Low-Cost Computing

Copyright © 2009 by Sander van Vugt

ISBN-13 (pbk): 978-1-4302-2441-9

ISBN-13 (electronic): 978-1-4302-2442-6

Printed and bound in the United States of America 9 8 7 6 5 4 3 2 1

Distributed to the book trade worldwide by Springer-Verlag New York, Inc., 233 Spring Street, 6th Floor, New York, NY 10013. Phone 1-800-SPRINGER, fax 201-348-4505, e-mail orders-ny@springer-sbm.com, or visit http://www.springeronline.com.

For information on translations, please contact Apress directly at 2855 Telegraph Avenue, Suite 600, Berkeley, CA 94705. Phone 510-549-5930, fax 510-549-5939, e-mail info@apress.com, or visit http://www.apress.com.

This book is dedicated to my beautiful family: Florence, Franck, and Alex

—Sander van Vugt

Contents at a Glance

Contents

About the Author

 **Sander van Vugt** is an independent Linux trainer, author, and technical consultant living in the Netherlands. He has written over 40 books so far, including his well-received *Beginning the Linux Command Line*. Sander is an acknowledged expert on matters of Linux high availability, performance, and storage-related issues, and a frequent speaker at Linux conferences all over the world. Most of his work is related to the "big three" Linux server operating systems: Ubuntu Server, SUSE Linux Enterprise Server, and Red Hat. He is using Ubuntu Netbook Remix on his netbook.

About the Technical Reviewer

 **Trevor Parsons** has been using free software for a decade and was founding editor of the UK's *LinuxUser* magazine. When he's not writing, editing, and breaking computers, he sidelines as a drummer and fiddle player. Even then, he's always armed with an Ubuntu flash drive in his violin case.

Acknowledgments

This book wouldn't have reached the quality it currently has without the help of my editor, Duncan Parkes, and the excellent and very patient technical reviewer, Trevor Parsons.

Introduction

Netbooks have conquered the world in the past few years; and as that has happened, Linux has been adopted at a larger scale as well. The reasons are obvious: Linux is a very versatile operating system that easily fits the needs of modern computing. That's also why Linux is installed on every computer type you can imagine.

Linux comes in different versions; Ubuntu currently is the most important, because you can get it for free and it's extremely user friendly. The options you need are never far from hand, and Ubuntu's possibilities seem endless. Since 2009, Ubuntu has offered a special Ubuntu Netbook Remix edition, with the aim of making your netbook experience more enjoyable. This book covers all you need to know about this netbook release of Ubuntu.

In this book, you learn how to work with Ubuntu Netbook Remix on your netbook. Chapter 1 covers how to install it. This chapter is followed by one that describes how Ubuntu Netbook Remix is organized; it teaches you how to perform common tasks and introduces this user-friendly software distribution. Given the nature of the netbook, the third chapter probably is the most important: it teaches you how to get connected to the Internet and other networks. You learn not only how to connect using your wireless network adapter, but also how to get connected to a 3G network. Chapter 4 teaches you which tools and programs are included with Ubuntu to work on the Internet. You learn how to read and send e-mail, browse the Web, optimize the browser, and perform other common Internet-related tasks. In Chapters 5 and 6, you learn how to work with different digital media on your netbook and how to perform office tasks using the Open Office suite. The last two chapters are dedicated to configuring and administering your netbook.

CHAPTER 1

■■■

Installing Ubuntu on a netbook

So you've bought a netbook computer, and you want to install Ubuntu on it. Good idea! In this chapter, you'll learn everything you need to know to get going with Ubuntu on the netbook:

- Netbook particularities

- The netbook and Linux

- Preparing for the installation

- Performing the installation

Netbook Particularities

A *netbook* is a particular kind of computer. It's small, cheap, and extremely portable, but the hardware is somewhat different from that used in a normal laptop. These differences make working with a netbook a unique computing experience. The disparities occur at the following levels:

- *A netbook uses a special kind of CPU*: At the moment, almost all netbook computers use the Intel Atom processor (but that may change in the near future). That means you shouldn't install just anything on a netbook you need a special version of the operating system you want to install.

- *The screen is small*: Most netbooks have a 9- or 10-inch screen. This is large enough to do your work; but the resolution is usually lower than you're used to, so you'll notice that programs don't look the way they normally do. Your operating system needs to be able to handle that difference in screen size.

- *Available disk space is limited*: Many netbooks work with flash memory, and often no more than about 16 GB (sometimes less) of disk space is available. Hence, you need to take care what you install—and there is currently no room to put your entire DVD collection on your netbook.

- *There's no optical drive*: To keep the netbook portable, an optical drive normally isn't installed. That means you can't install anything from a CD-ROM unless you buy an additional external optical drive.

- *You can use many options to connect*: These include a LAN interface for a wired network and a Wi-Fi interface for wireless connections. In addition, a Bluetooth device helps you connect to a peripheral device such as your mobile telephone, which lets you use that device as a modem to connect to the Internet.

Despite the differences, many things on a netbook are the same as on a laptop. Because you can install all the common operating systems on your netbook, you can also install familiar applications on it. But remember, resources are limited. The CPU in a netbook isn't a number-cruncher, so you shouldn't use it to render videos, for instance. For daily computing activities, such as connecting to the Internet and working on office documents, however, the netbook is an excellent choice.

Before I talk about using Ubuntu on a netbook, I should discuss exactly what' I'm talking about, because there are different brands of netbooks. It all began with Asus Eee PC. This was developed as a small netbook, typically with a 9" screen (in the beginning it only was 7"); it has no rotating hard disk but uses flash memory instead. Asus can be considered the inventor of the netbook, with the result that specific netbook distributions often are developed with the Asus netbook in mind.

The second important player is Acer, with the Aspire One netbook. This netbook looks a little more like a normal laptop; it has a rotating hard disk, and the standard screen size is 10" instead of 9".

Many other companies have entered the netbook market. But Asus and Acer can still be considered the leaders, especially from the perspective of the Linux kernel. That means the netbook Linux distros that you download from the Internet are most likely adjusted for one of these brands—and if you want to make your Linux netbook experience an easy one, it's a good idea to work with one of them.

The Netbook and Linux

Some netbooks come with Linux preinstalled, and others don't. If Linux is on your netbook, it can be any flavor. Many flavors of Linux (the so-called *distributions*) have a special version that is optimized to be used on a netbook. One of these is Ubuntu, which is currently the most popular Linux distribution on the planet.

Why Linux?

In addition to Linux, many netbook computers come with Windows preinstalled. You may wonder why you should bother switching to Linux. There are a few compelling reasons to do so, and they come down to one word: *freedom*. You should also consider the practical reasons, such as having an OS that isn't susceptible to malware and is much more up to date than Windows XP, which dates back to 2001.

Working with Linux means working in freedom. With Linux, you don't just get the operating system for free: you get your applications for free, as well. After installing Linux, you have a complete working environment on your computer. The OS lets you perform basic operations on your computer and also runs all the applications you need. And if ever you require an application that hasn't been installed by default, you can download it from the Internet—for free.

Linux has its strengths and its limitations. You can't run Windows applications out of the box (a solution called Wine helps you do so if you really want to). In the beginning, that may be difficult from time to time, because Linux applications are different from those in Windows. But that's why you bought this book; it will guide you through the most common Linux components and programs. In the end, you'll find Linux alternatives for your Windows applications. And you won't want to switch back to Windows.

Reasons Not to Use Linux

If you're used to Windows or Mac, you'll notice that Linux is different. You have to get used to the way things are done in a Linux environment, but that's what this book will help you with. This adjustment may be tough at times. It will also be fun. And after you've used Linux a couple of times, you'll notice that you're getting good at it. That's the moment when you start to like Linux and probably don't want to work with anything else.

One of the good things about working with Linux is that nearly everything is free. By default, Ubuntu comes with free components only. You'll find information about lots of free Linux alternatives in this book that are as good as the Windows programs and sometimes even better. If everything goes right, after reading this book, you won't need Windows anymore. You'll find that Ubuntu Netbook Remix is an excellent choice for your netbook. After you get used to the new desktop, you'll find that it's organized better than Windows. You'll rarely have to search for programs but will find everything from the easy-to-use, accessible desktop interface. Working with Ubuntu Netbook Remix is a convenient point-and-click experience.

■ **Tip** After reading this book, if you're still not convinced, no worries. Apress also has an excellent book on running Windows on a netbook (*Windows Netbooks: The Path to Low-Cost Computing*, by James Floyd Kelly).

Ubuntu and the Netbook

The world of Linux is fast changing. At the moment this book was written, several initiatives were available for running Ubuntu on a netbook:

- *Ubuntu Netbook Remix*: The official version of Ubuntu for use on a netbook. *Official* in this case means it's developed by Canonical, the company that has also developed the desktop version of Ubuntu Linux. The purpose of the Ubuntu Netbook Remix is to develop a product that can be installed by netbook manufacturers, such as Dell, with its Inspiron Mini 9 and 12 netbooks. However, you can also install it yourself. You can find more information about the Ubuntu Netbook Remix at http://www.canonical.com/projects/ubuntu/unr.

- *Eeebuntu*: An open source derivative from the normal desktop version of Ubuntu. It has no link with Canonical, the supporting organization behind Ubuntu. At the moment this was written, Eeebuntu had some issues with peripheral devices such as SD-card readers. Because Ubuntu Netbook Remix is now available (which wasn't the case when Eeebuntu was first released), there is no longer a good reason to use Eeebuntu. But if you want to give it a try, you can download Eeebuntu from http://www.eeebuntu.org

- *Easy Peasy*: Formerly known as Ubuntu Eee; an open source initiative to deliver Ubuntu for the netbook. This distribution looks like Ubuntu Netbook Remix. Its kernel supports most hardware, and therefore it's an excellent choice to install on your netbook. It also includes some programs that you won't find in a typical open source environment, such as Skype, Flash, Picasa, and a number of codecs. Initially, Easy Peasy had the best hardware support; but because Ubuntu Netbook Remix is now available, you probably won't need Easy Peasy. You can download it from http://www.geteasypeasy.com.

Which Ubuntu?

From the information so far, you've learned that different versions of Ubuntu are available for the netbook. I can't cover them all in this book; and in the end, it doesn't matter which one you install. You'll use the applications that are offered by your Ubuntu netbook version, so only the applications really matter. The most important applications that are available in all Ubuntu netbook versions are as follows:

- *Web browser*: Firefox 3
- *E-mail client*: Evolution
- *Instant messenger*: Pidgin
- *Media player*: Rhythmbox
- *e-book reader*: FBReader
- *Photo viewer*: F-Spot
- *Office suite*: OpenOffice.org

For this book, I did need to make a choice. Because the official version of Ubuntu supported by Canonical has the best chances for the future, I'm covering installation of the Ubuntu Netbook Remix, which you can find at `http://www.canonical.com/projects/ubuntu/unr`. If you choose to use a different Ubuntu netbook distribution, that's fine, but you'll need to look up the installation instructions on the Internet.

■ **Note** By the time you read this, it's more than likely that several netbook computers will come with Ubuntu Netbook Remix preinstalled. If this is the case, you can go directly to the next chapter and skip the installation discussion.

Preparing for the Ubuntu Netbook Remix Installation

On most netbooks, Windows is preinstalled. The first thing to do is replace that with Ubuntu Netbook Remix. Before you begin to install Ubuntu Netbook Remix, check that your netbook meets the following minimum requirements suggested by the developers:

- Intel Atom processor
- 512 MB RAM
- 4 GB flash disk or hard disk

For a more detailed list of compatible hardware, check `https://wiki.ubuntu.com/HardwareSupport/Machines/Netbooks`, which groups hardware into tiers of compatibility.

To install Ubuntu Netbook Remix, you need two things to start with. Because a netbook doesn't have an optical drive, you can't install from CD or DVD, unless you have an external optical drive that you can connect to a USB port on your computer. If this is the case, you can burn the installation image to a CD and start the installation from there. Skip to the next section if you can do that.

If you don't have an optical drive that you can connect to your computer, you need to download an installation image, copy it to a USB key, and boot from the USB key. The following procedure describes how to download the installation image and put it on your USB key. I'll cover both the Windows-based installation and the Linux-based installation, so it doesn't matter from which operating system you perform this procedure:

■ **Note** This part of the book is about information that changes (very) fast. I recommend that you check `https://wiki.ubuntu.com/UNR` for the most up-to-date information if the steps described in this chapter no longer work.

---

1. Download the installation image from `http://cdimage.ubuntu.com/ubuntu-netbook-remix/daily-live/current`. At this website, you'll find a list of files; look for the file that has the extension .img. In my case, the file name is `jaunty-netbook-remix-i386.img`; for future Ubuntu versions, this name will certainly be different. Save the file to your computer's desktop.

2. Write the image you just downloaded to a USB key. Make sure you have a USB key with a minimum size of 1 GB available. Also make sure there is no important data on the USB key, because writing the image to the USB key will remove all other data.

Writing the Image to a USB Key in Windows

If you're working in Windows, continue with these steps. Otherwise, skip to "Writing the Image to a USB Key in Linux":

1. On Windows, you need the flashnul tool. You can download it from `http://shounen.ru/soft/flashnul/`. This site is in Russian, with one exception: the Download hyperlink. Click it to obtain the most recent version of flashnul. Download the file to your desktop, unzip it, and copy it to the `Windows\System32` directory.

2. Attach the USB key to your Windows computer, and use the `flashnul -p` command to list all your USB devices. Note the number of the physical USB drive, and next use the following command:

   `flashnul <devicenumber> -L \path\to\unr.img`

   Note that in this command, you need to use the device number you obtained from the `flashnul -p` command. Next, using the option `-L`, you specify the exact location where you can find the image file. Also make sure you replace `unr.img` with the exact name of the image. Wait until the image file is copied to the USB key, which completes this procedure for Windows users.

Writing the Image to a USB Key in Linux

If you're working in Linux, follow these steps:

1. You can open a command-line interface now—unless you're doing this on an Ubuntu machine, in which case you should check out "Writing the Image to a USB Key with Ubuntu Image Writer." This is different for each Linux distribution; but given that you want to do this on Linux, you probably know how to open a command-line interface.

2. Make sure the USB key is attached to your Linux computer. Next, using root permissions, use the `lsscsi` command to find out the device name of your USB-key (try `sudo lsscsi` if just `lsscsi` doesn't work). On many modern computers, it will be `/dev/sdb`; but you need to be sure before proceeding, because if you use the wrong device name, you risk losing all the data on your computer's hard drive. In the output of `lsscsi`, you'll normally recognize the brand of the USB drive manufacturer. Only proceed if you know for sure how to address your USB device!

3. Use the `dd` command to write the image to your USB key:

    ```
    dd if=/home/user/Desktop/jaunty-netbook-remix-i386.img of=/dev/sdb bs=4096
    ```

    After this command has completed, you can remove the USB device from your computer. Your USB installation stick is now ready.

Writing the Image to a USB Key with Ubuntu Image Writer

The procedure described in the previous section is doable but not easy. There is an easy procedure as well, which uses a graphical program called USB Image Writer. This procedure works only from an Ubuntu computer. If you're using Ubuntu already, download USB image Writer, and install it. Then, open Applications ➤ Accessories ➤ Image Writer, put the USB key in a USB port on your computer, select the downloaded image, select the target device, and click Write to Device.

Performing the Installation

Now that you've prepared the USB stick for the installation, it's time to start the installation. Make sure the stick is attached to a USB port of your netbook, and then push the power button to switch the netbook on. When it boots, interrupt the boot procedure. On the Acer Aspire One, for instance, you can press the F12 key to bring up a boot device menu; on the Asus Eee Pc, press the Escape key for the same purpose. The following procedure describes all steps you have to pass through from here:

1. After you boot from the USB stick, you see a menu from which you can select the language you want to work with (see Figure 1-1). The mouse doesn't work on this initial menu, so you need to use the keyboard to make your selections. English is selected by default, so if you want to install in English, press Enter. This brings you to the main screen of the Ubuntu Netbook Remix installation program (see Figure 1-2).

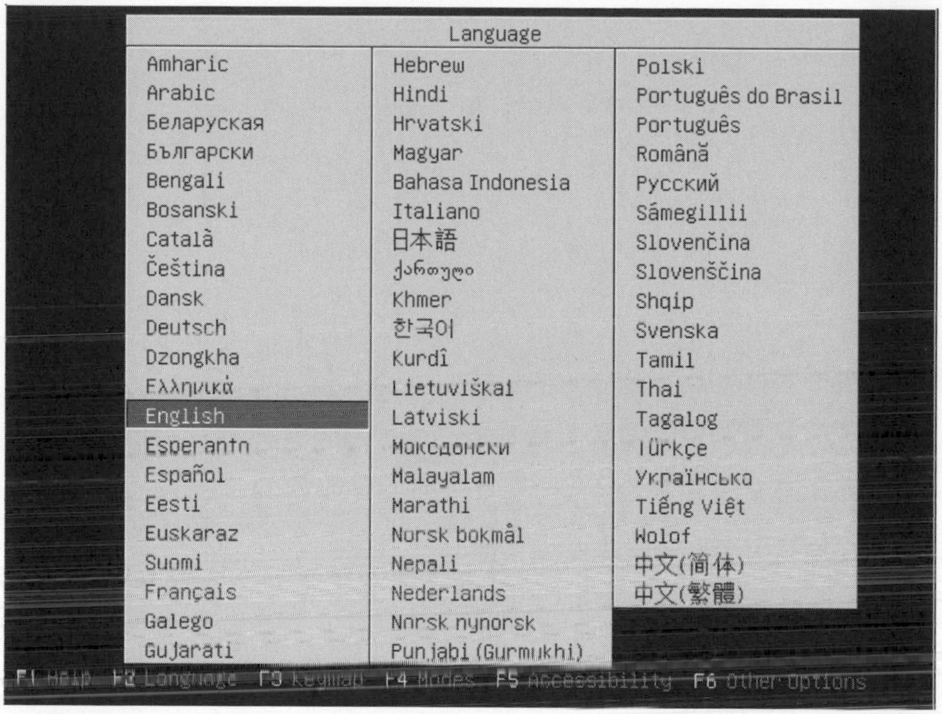

Language		
Amharic	Hebrew	Polski
Arabic	Hindi	Português do Brasil
Беларуская	Hrvatski	Português
Български	Magyar	Română
Bengali	Bahasa Indonesia	Русский
Bosanski	Italiano	Sámegillii
Català	日本語	Slovenčina
Čeština	ქართული	Slovenščina
Dansk	Khmer	Shqip
Deutsch	한국어	Svenska
Dzongkha	Kurdî	Tamil
Ελληνικά	Lietuviškai	Thai
English	Latviski	Tagalog
Esperanto	Македонски	Türkçe
Español	Malayalam	Українська
Eesti	Marathi	Tiếng Việt
Euskaraz	Norsk bokmål	Wolof
Suomi	Nepali	中文(简体)
Français	Nederlands	中文(繁體)
Galego	Norsk nynorsk	
Gujarati	Punjabi (Gurmukhi)	

F1 Help F2 Language F3 Keymap F4 Modes F5 Accessibility F6 Other Options

Figure 1-1. Ubuntu Netbook Remix offers support for a number of languages.

7

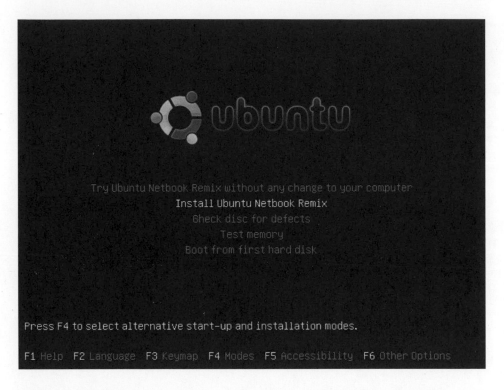

Figure 1-2. On the main screen, select the Install Ubuntu Netbook Remix option.

2. If you're not working with a U.S. keyboard layout, press F3 as well, so you can select the proper keyboard layout.

■ **Tip** Still not sure that you want to wipe Windows and replace it with Ubuntu Netbook Remix? In that case, from the boot menu, select the first option, which lets you try Ubuntu Netbook Remix without installing it.

---

3. From the installation menu, select Install Ubuntu Netbook Remix, and press Enter. This starts the installation procedure. You'll have to wait a minute until the installation program loads.

4. When the program has loaded, you see the first step of the seven-step installation procedure (see Figure 1-3). Select the installation language (again). In this case, select English, and then click Forward to proceed.

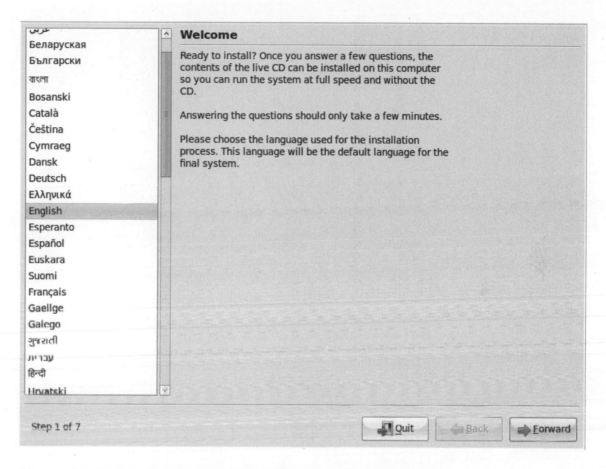

Figure 1-3. *In the first screen of seven, select English as your installation language.*

5. You now see a map of the globe. Click this map to select your location, or use the Region and City drop-down menus to specify exactly where on the globe you are. Then, click Forward to continue (see Figure 1-4).

Figure 1-4. *To indicate the part of the world you're in, click the globe or select your region and city from the drop-down menus.*

6.   The installer proposes a keyboard layout based on your location. The program may be wrong, so test whether all the keys on your keyboard work properly. If they don't, select the keyboard layout you need. If you're not sure, USA International is always a good choice. If you have three symbols listed on the numeric keys, be sure you select the AltGr dead keys option. Test if it works as it's supposed to, and then click Forward to go to the next step.

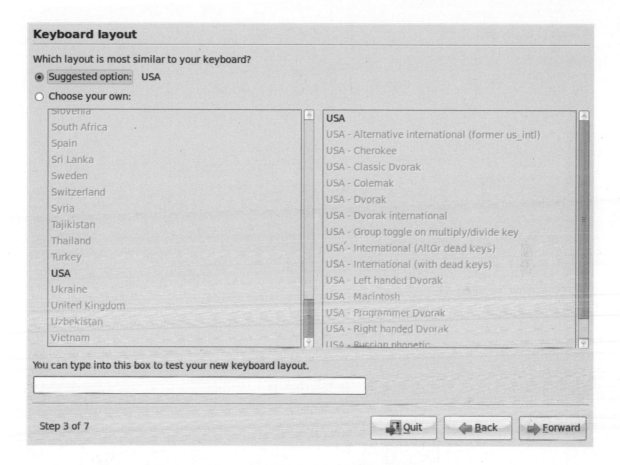

Figure 1-5. *Based on your geographical settings, a keyboard layout is suggested.*

7.   At this point, the installer analyzes your hard disk. If it finds another operating system already installed, it usually suggests that you install Ubuntu and the other operating system side by side, allowing you to boot either of them. If this is what you want, select the Install Them Side By Side option. If you only want Ubuntu and nothing else, select Use the Entire Disk. I'll assume that you want to use the entire hard disk. Make your choice, and click Forward.

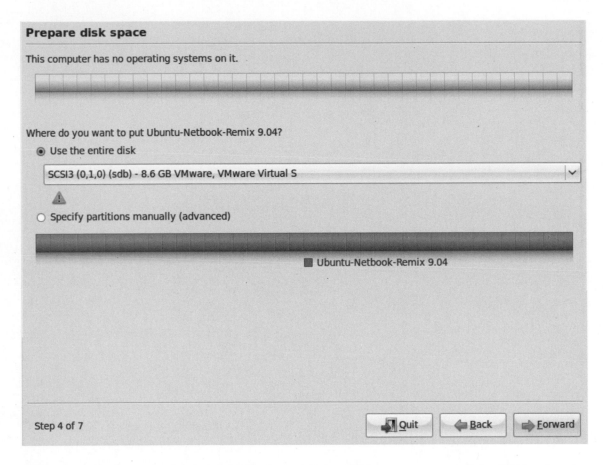

Figure 1-6. To make sure only Ubuntu Netbook Remix is installed on your computer's hard disk, select the Use the Entire Disk option.

8. Now you need to identify yourself. (Don't worry, this information isn't sent anywhere.) Based on that identification, a username is created. You also need to provide a password for your user name. It's a good idea to choose a password that isn't in the dictionary and is at least eight characters long. If you don't do that, you'll get a warning, but you still can enter the password. You also need to enter a name for the computer; this name is used to identify the computer on the network. Last, specify whether you want to log in automatically or whether you want extra security, which means you'll always need a password before login. The latter is more secure, because it ensures that no one can access your data without entering the password first. After you enter all your credentials, click Forward.

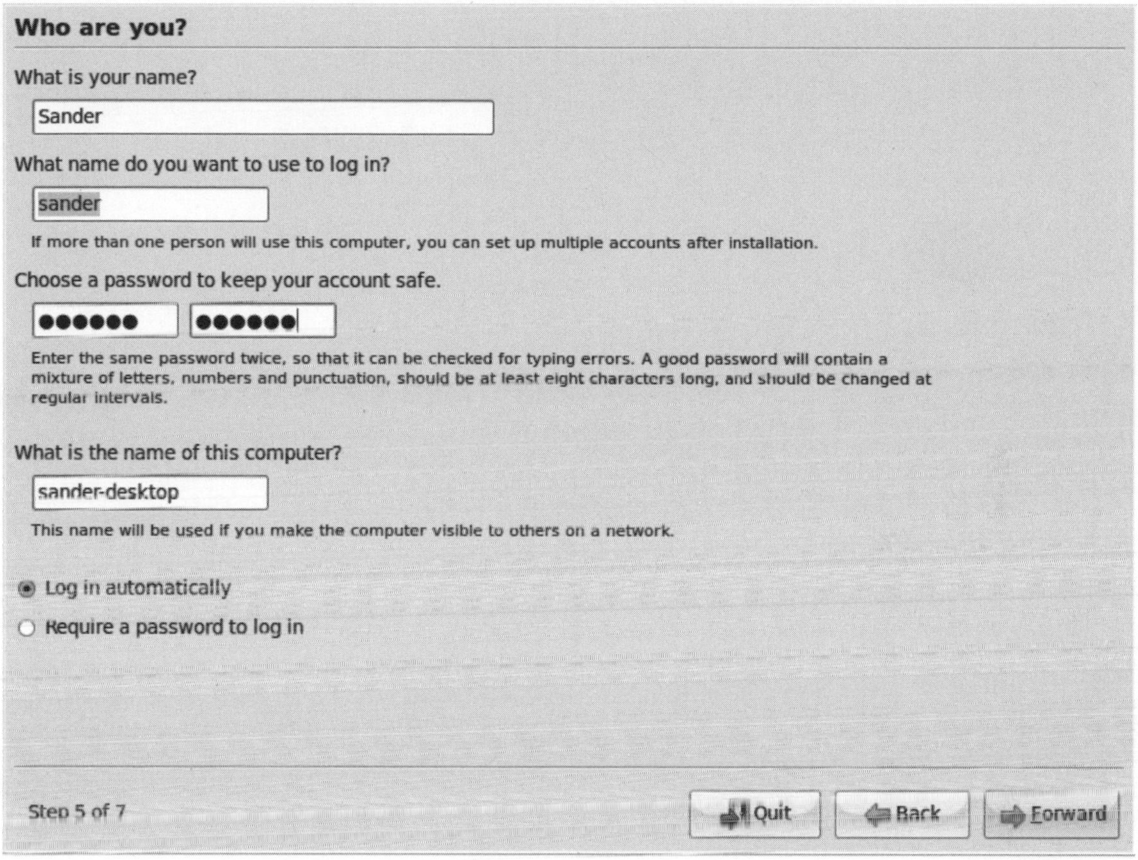

Who are you?

What is your name?

```
Sander
```

What name do you want to use to log in?

```
sander
```

If more than one person will use this computer, you can set up multiple accounts after installation.

Choose a password to keep your account safe.

```
●●●●●●        ●●●●●●
```

Enter the same password twice, so that it can be checked for typing errors. A good password will contain a mixture of letters, numbers and punctuation, should be at least eight characters long, and should be changed at regular intervals.

What is the name of this computer?

```
sander-desktop
```

This name will be used if you make the computer visible to others on a network.

⦿ Log in automatically

◯ Require a password to log in

Step 5 of 7   🠻 Quit   ⬅ Back   ➡ Forward

Figure 1-7. To identify yourself, create a user account and password.

9. The next (and last) screen of the installation wizard provides an overview of all the selections you've made (see Figure 1-8). Two advanced options are also available: you can reach them by clicking the Advanced button. One option lets you specify where to install the program that allows you to boot Linux (the boot loader); you shouldn't change this unless you know exactly what you're doing. You can also enter the IP address and port number of an HTTP proxy that you may need to access the Internet. Click OK to close the Advanced window, and then click Install to start the installation. Your installation settings are written to hard disk, and all the software is copied. This takes several minutes.

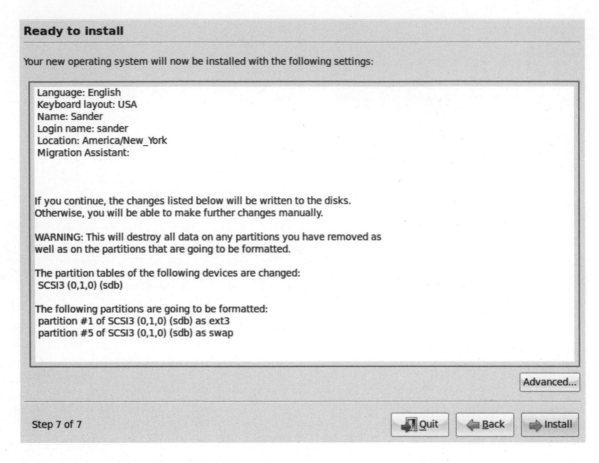

Ready to install

Your new operating system will now be installed with the following settings:

Language: English
Keyboard layout: USA
Name: Sander
Login name: sander
Location: America/New_York
Migration Assistant:

If you continue, the changes listed below will be written to the disks.
Otherwise, you will be able to make further changes manually.

WARNING: This will destroy all data on any partitions you have removed as
well as on the partitions that are going to be formatted.

The partition tables of the following devices are changed:
SCSI3 (0,1,0) (sdb)

The following partitions are going to be formatted:
partition #1 of SCSI3 (0,1,0) (sdb) as ext3
partition #5 of SCSI3 (0,1,0) (sdb) as swap

Advanced...

Step 7 of 7   Quit   Back   Install

Figure 1-8. On the last screen of the installation program, you get an overview of the settings you've selected.

10. After the installation is complete, you see a prompt to restart your computer. Do that now to get access to the new operating system on your netbook. Before you restart the computer, be sure the USB installation key is detached; then, press Enter to continue.

Summary

The most popular Linux distribution is also available for netbooks. Different open source initiatives are available to deliver Ubuntu for netbooks; of these, Ubuntu Netbook Remix seems destined to become the winner. In this chapter, you've learned where to get it and how to install it. In the next chapter, you'll learn how to get your everyday computer work done using Ubuntu Netbook Remix.

■ ■ ■

CHAPTER 2

Starting to Use Ubuntu Netbook Remix

Now that you've installed Ubuntu Netbook Remix, it's time to do something with it. I'll assume this is your first time using Ubuntu or Linux, so in this chapter you'll learn the basics you need to know to be able to work with Linux. The following topics are covered:

- Exploring the desktop
- Using Nautilus to work with files
- Attaching external storage
- Setting desktop preferences

A Radical New Interface

You'll see immediately after you start Ubuntu Netbook Remix (UNR) that it's a completely different operating system with a radical new desktop. UNR tries to break with the classical idea of a computer desktop, which is a place where you put files. Instead, it offers an interface that helps you find the application you need as fast as possible.

Even compared to Ubuntu on a regular desktop computer, UNR looks different. The redesigned interface tries to work with resources in the most convenient way, because the available screen space is limited. To let you fit as much as you possibly can on the screen, the interface uses tabs to organize your work. You'll also notice that programs aren't started in a window with decorations round the outside, but go directly to full screen. This ensures that you get the best possible work environment. Figure 2-1 shows the netbook launcher, which is UNR's home screen.

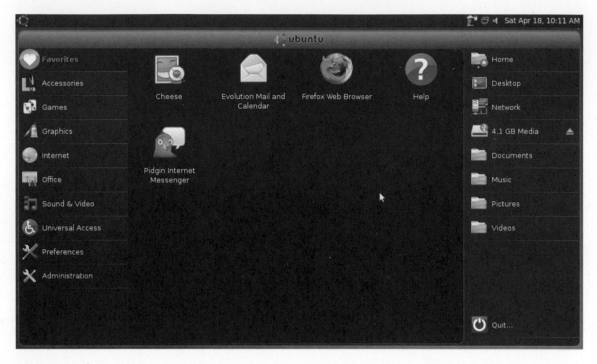

Figure 2-1. *The UNR interface is organized to let you work with the limited desktop size in the most efficient way.*

Changing Settings from the Panel

At the top of the screen is a black horizontal strip with the Ubuntu logo in the left corner. This is the *panel*. After you start programs, icons appear in the upper-left corner, next to the Ubuntu icon. Every active program is represented by a little icon that you can click to regain access to the program. Clicking the Ubuntu icon takes you back to the home screen.

Next, in the upper-right corner, you can see the current battery status, the current network status, an icon that helps you adjust the volume on your sound card, and the current date and time. If you move your mouse cursor over any of these, you see a current status summary; if you click an icon once, you get access to a quick menu that lets you perform tasks related to the program. For instance, Figure 2-2 shows what you see if you click the date-and-time indicator.

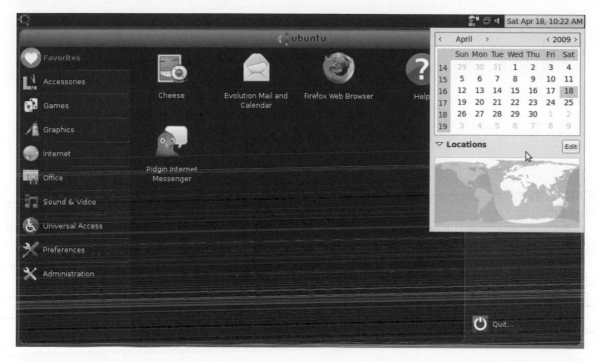

Figure 2-2. Click the panel icons in the upper-right corner to access more information and options.

Most panel applets on UNR share the same elements and work in similar ways. If you double-click any icon, a program window opens that offers the corresponding functionality. Advanced and more detailed configuration options are often available via other buttons on the menus or button bar.

The panel icons in the upper-right corner also work like this. For instance, the appointment and tasks applet shown in Figure 2-2 (which you access by clicking it) lets you easily navigate to your appointments on any given day by clicking the date in the calendar view. Doing so opens the Evolution application, which you use to manage appointments and tasks in more detail.

If you want to do advanced things, such as change your current location on the globe, click the drop-down arrow (the triangle) next to Locations (shown in Figure 2-2) to open a map of the earth; you can now click the Edit button to specify configuration options. In this case, the window shown in Figure 2-3 opens; here, you can use the three tabs to specify general settings, add locations, or configure weather settings. One main menu item lets you open submenu items in different windows.

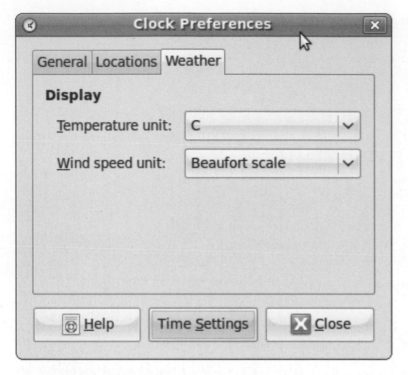

Figure 2-3. *From the main configuration menu of panel applets, often several sub menus are available.*

Also notice the Help button that is available in almost all submenus. Clicking this button provides more details about how to perform the current task.

Many applications on your Ubuntu netbook work this way. The primary functionality is offered from the main application window, and you can access other functions by selecting items from tabs, buttons, and drop-down menus.

■ **Tip** Some Netbooks have only one mouse button. Even if that's the case, you can still right-click. The Acer Aspire One, for instance, has one long mouse button. Press the left side of this button for a left-click, or press the right side of the button for a right-click. It's that easy.

The Launcher: Your Netbook's Home Screen

The main part of the netbook interface is used by the *launcher*. It's composed of application groups on the left, application icons belonging to the selected group in the middle, and Places tabs on the right, which give you access to folders, network locations, and flash drives on your computer.

To find the application you need, you start with the application groups, which divide the applications you use into categories. These application menus and their contents are as follows:

- *Favorites*: You can put your favorite applications in this group. Some applications are there by default, like the Evolution Mail and Calendar program, the Firefox web browser, and the Pidgin instant messaging program. It's easy to add other applications: go to the application menu that includes the item you want to add, right-click the application's icon, and select Add to Favorites (see Figure 2-4). The application is added to the Favorites menu immediately.

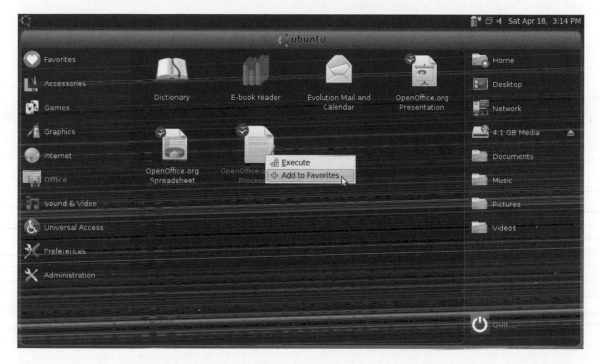

Figure 2-4. Right-click an application icon and select Add to Favorites to add it to the Favorites menu.

- *Accessories*: In the Accessories menu (see Figure 8-5), you'll find some useful applications. For instance, the Add Remove applet lets you install new applications (I'll cover adding and removing applications in more detail in Chapter 8). If your default language has special characters that you can't find on the keyboard, you can use the Character Map. Of special interest for advanced Linux users is the Terminal window: it offers shell access to the Linux operating system, which lets you accomplish some of the most complicated system administration tasks.

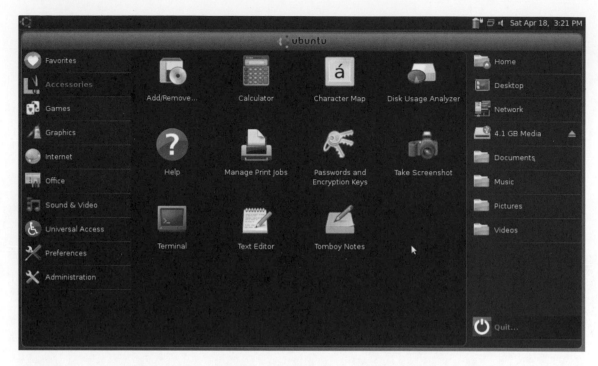

Figure 2-5. *The Accessories menu—a versatile Swiss Army knife of handy utilities*

- *Games*: Do I need to explain what you find here? Probably not. The Games menu hosts a surprisingly large collection of computer games, including Solitaire, Chess, Mines, and Sudoku. You'll always find something to do.

- *Graphics*: This menu has to do with graphical applications. After a default installation, you'll find three of them. First is Cheese webcam booth. If you've always dreamed of becoming a movie star, you can use this little program to take pictures and shoot movies from your netbook's webcam (see Figure 2-6). Next is the F-Spot photo manager, which you can use to manage and to some degree optimize pictures. Last is OpenOffice.org Draw, the drawing program that is included in OpenOffice.org.

Figure 2-6. Using Cheese, you can take pictures and shoot movies from your netbook's webcam.

- *Internet*: Here you find three programs that help you communicate on the Internet. First Evolution, the default mail program; you can even use it to fetch mail from an Exchange mail server. Next is the famous Firefox web browser, which probably doesn't need any further introduction. Last but not least is Pidgin, an amazing instant-messenger client capable of connecting to your contacts on AIM, MSN, Yahoo!, XMPP, ICQ, IRC, and many other IM networks.

- *Office*: This group contains version 3 of the free office suite, OpenOffice.org. The default installation includes a word processor, a presentation program, and a spreadsheet program. You'll also find a dictionary and an e-book reader.

- *Sound & Video*: If your netbook has a hard disk, you'll appreciate the option to watch movies and listen to sound. To do this, the Sound & Video menu offers you Movie Player, the Rhythmbox music player, and Sound Recorder, which lets you record your own sound.

- *Universal Access*: If you have problems working with a keyboard, the CellWriter application in this menu gives you the ability to work with alternative input devices.

- *Preferences*: Using the programs that are offered in the Preferences menu (see Figure 2-7), you can set up your netbook just the way you like it. For instance, you can enter personal information, modify the default appearance, configure a printer, and much, much more. Later in this chapter, in the section "Setting Preferences," you'll learn about some of the possibilities that are offered here.

Figure 2-7. In the Preferences menu, you'll find different applications that allow you to personalize your netbook.

- *Administration*: Last but not least is the Administration menu. Here you find some of the more complex administration utilities. These settings are typically used to optimize your netbook experience or use your netbook to perform administration tasks for other users. For instance, these programs let you monitor the network, configure user accounts, and specify how updates should be handled. These aren't typical tasks that everyone has to worry about! In Chapter 8, you'll learn about the most important of these administration tasks.

Access to Documents and Files

On the right side of the screen, the Places section gives you access to documents and storage on your netbook. You can access your personal documents by clicking Home, access devices on the network, or access files and folders on removable storage media.

Working with removable storage isn't hard: you just connect the removable storage to your computer, and it appears automatically in the Places section on the UNR desktop. For instance, Figure 2-8 shows that a 4.1 GB media device is attached to the computer.

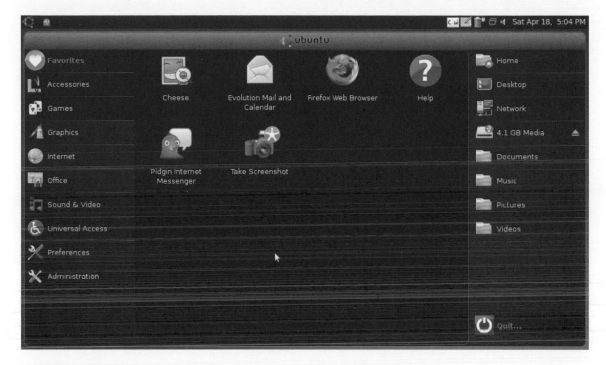

Figure 2-8. When you connect removable storage to your computer, it appears automatically in the Places section.

To see what is on a plugged-in removable storage device, click the link to the media. Doing so opens the File Browser, which you'll learn more about in the next section. If you've just inserted a removable storage device, it's even easier: the File Browser automatically opens and shows you the device's contents. Figure 2-9 shows this application. If the removable storage contains documents in a supported format, you automatically see previews of those documents. When you're finished working with your documents, you can close the File Browser to return to the main screen.

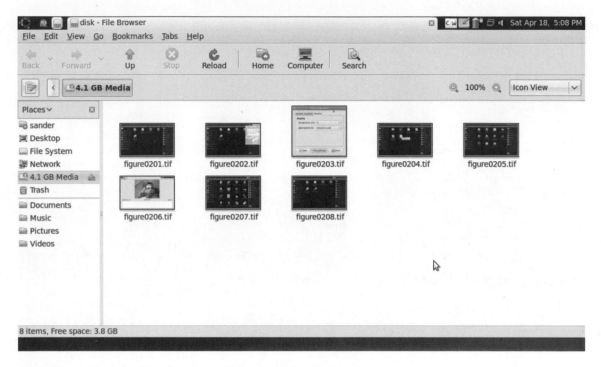

Figure 2-9. When you click the removable storage, the File Browser opens.

When you finish working on a removable storage device, you can't just remove the device—you must tell the netbook that you're going to disconnect it. To do this, from the launcher screen, click the Eject symbol next to the removable storage. The removable storage will be disconnected (*unmounted* in Linux slang). You can tell it's disconnected when the eject symbol disappears. At this point, it's safe to disconnect the removable storage device.

Using the File Browser

As you've read previously, in the Places section on the right side of the launcher screen, you can access your files and folders. This section provides shortcuts to your home folder; the Desktop icon, which gives you an overview of icons on your computer desktop; the computers in your network environment, and the Documents, Music, Pictures, and Videos folders in your home directory. You can use any of these to access files in these folders.

■ **Note** Linux people like to talk about directories instead of folders. Just for your information, they're the same thing. What most people now refer to as a *folder* was called a *directory* in the early years of computing.

To work with files, you need to use the File Browser. Click the Home icon to get to your home directory. You see your personal directory and all the files and folders that exist in that directory. Assuming that you've performed a normal installation, it looks like Figure 2-10.

Figure 2-10. The contents of your home directory

From here, you can do anything to files. Follow these steps to make a new file and copy it to another location on your computer:

1. In the home directory view in Figure 2-10, right-click anywhere in the window. From the menu that appears, select Create Document ➤ Empty File, which creates a new file (see Figure 2-11).

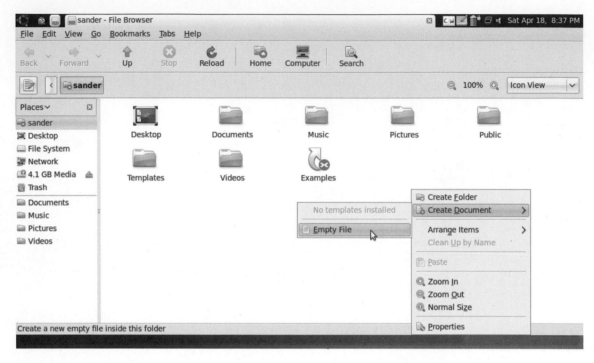

Figure 2-11. Right-click the background of the File Browser to see available options.

2. A new icon is added to the contents of your home directory. The name that is
    added to this file by default is new file. This file name is highlighted; you can
    type a new name over the highlighted text. Do so now, and press Enter to
    complete the renaming of the file.

    At this point, you've created a new file, but it's not in the right location (see
    Figure 2-12). Your home directory contains several ready-made folders, each
    for a specific kind of file. You need to move the new file to the Documents
    folder, which is the appropriate location for new documents.

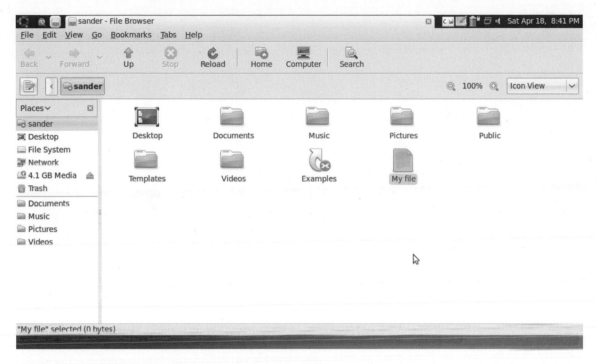

Figure 2-12. Make sure each document is in the right folder.

3. To move a file, several options are available. All of these are common to other operating systems as well:

Drag the file, and drop it into the folder where you want it. This must be one of the folders listed at left part on the screen or that you see anywhere else in the current File Browser view.

Right-click the file, and select Cut to move it or Copy to make a copy of it. Next, navigate to the folder where you want to place the file, right-click in that folder, and select Paste. Doing so puts a copy of the file in the new location.

Select the file, and select Edit ➤ Cut from the File Browser menu. Browse to the location where you want to put a copy of the file, and choose Paste from the File Browser's Edit menu.

Exploring the Root File System

In UNR, you'll work with files in your home folder most of the time. These are the files you see when you click the icon that has your name on it in the File Browser. But UNR includes more than your personal files. The operating system creates a bunch of directories when you install it. This is the system environment, where you won't have anything useful to do if you're a normal user. If you're curious, you can look around. Just be aware that, as in Windows, you normally won't work here—but it doesn't hurt to know what's going on. You can access these directories by clicking the File System link in the File Browser (see Figure 2-13).

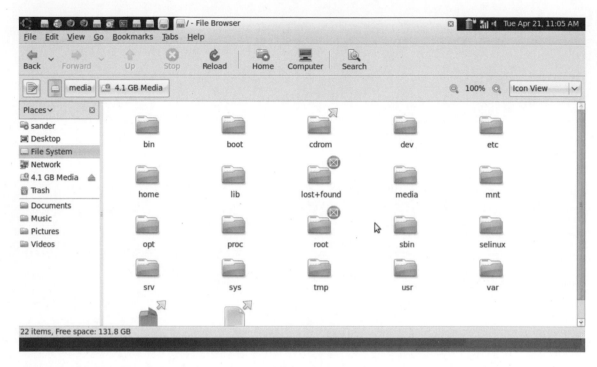

Figure 2-13. Click the File System link to access files in the root directory of your computer.

As you can see, multiple directories are available from the root of the file system. The good news is that normally, you don't need to do anything with these directories. All the devices you connect to your netbook appear automatically in the bar at the left in the File Browser, and you can access files on the devices directly from this bar. You need the directories in your system's root only if you want to perform system-administration tasks. In all other situations, it's a good idea to avoid this directory, to prevent you from changing important system settings by accident.

Managing Trash

As long as you work from the File Browser interface, files that you delete are placed in the trash bin automatically. To remove a file from the trash, right-click the file and select Restore from the menu. Doing so puts the file back at its original location (see Figure 2-14).

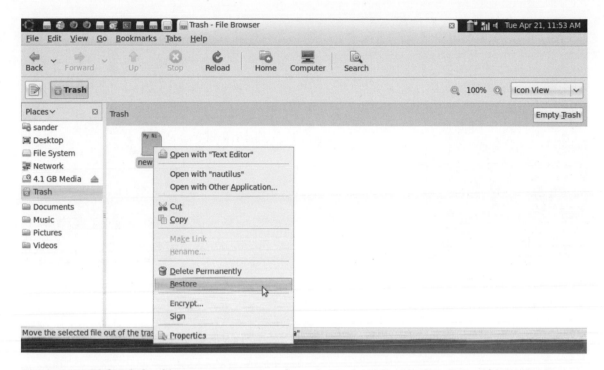

Figure 2-14. Right-click a file you want to restore from the trash, and next select Restore from the menu.

Alternatively, you can remove an individual file permanently from your computer's hard drive by right-clicking the file and selecting Delete Permanently. To remove all the files in the trash at once, click the Empty Trash button in the upper-right corner of the Trash folder.

Specifying File Properties

From the File Browser interface, you can specify advanced file properties. These properties can help make it easier to work with files. To set file properties, right-click the file in the File Browser interface, and select Properties from the menu. Doing so opens the window shown in Figure 2-15.

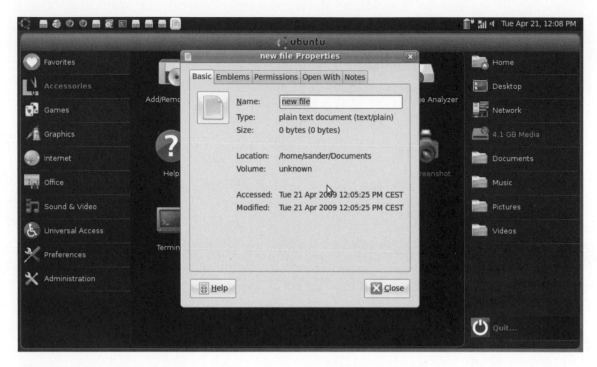

Figure 2-15. *The Properties interface allows you to set additional file properties.*

If you select multiple files, you can change the properties for all of them at once. First, make your selection by clicking and dragging the mouse cursor over the files you want to modify, or by clicking the names of the individual files while holding the Ctrl key. Next, right-click the selection, and select Properties from the menu.

The Basic tab of the Properties interface shows statistics about the file, such as its name (which you can change here), its type and size, and the time the file was last accessed and modified.

On the Emblems tab, you can choose from different icons to connect to the file. These icons make it easier for you to recognize files of a certain type. For instance, you can select the Urgent icon to mark all files that require urgent action, or any other icon to mark files from a specific category (see Figure 2-16).

Figure 2-16. Icons let you mark files of a certain type to recognize them more easily.

To secure access to a file, you can grant permissions. The default settings are easy to understand: the user who creates a file is the only one who can read and write to the file. Other users are only allowed to read the file. If you share your netbook with others, and you don't want them to have permission to open certain files and read them, you can take away the access permission. To do this, in the Properties window, open the Permissions tab; then, select None from the Others drop-down list (see Figure 2-17).

■ **Note** To set permissions for a folder and have them apply to everything in the folder, click the Apply Permissions to Enclosed Files button.

Figure 2-17. *If you want to be sure you're the only one who can access a file, set the permissions for others to None.*

In addition to the basic access permissions that determine who can read and write to files, Linux files have an execute permission. If your file is a program file or script, and you need to run it, you must make sure the Allow Executing File as a Program option is selected. By default, this option is set for all files that need it; but in some cases, you'll need to set it yourself.

The next useful file property is on the Open With tab. Here, you can specify which application to use to open a file. When the correct application is listed, you can double-click a file in the File Browser to open it with that application. By default, all applications that make sense for the selected file type are listed. This happens based on the file extension. For instance, if a file has the extension .txt, it's probably a text file, and it makes sense to open it with a text editor or with the OpenOffice.org word processor (see Figure 2-18). If you think another application should be listed to open this file, click Add on the Open With tab to select that application from the list of available applications on your computer.

Figure 2-18. On the Open With tab, you specify which application to use to open a given file type.

Last is the Notes tab. On this tab, you can put your own notes to be associated with a file. If a file has notes, the File Browser displays a small notes symbol on the file's icon.

Setting Preferences

Now, back to the launcher home screen. The Preferences tab gives you options that help you set up your system the way you want it. Some of these are related to appearance, and others provide useful information about your computer. In this section, you'll learn about some of the most interesting preferences. Note that I won't cover settings related to network connectivity or connected hardware; you'll find more information about those in Chapters 3 and 8.

About Me

A netbook is a very small computer—so small that it's easy to forget it, or throw it away by accident. If that happens, you can hope that someone honest finds it. To help this person send the netbook back to you, you can enter personal information under About Me. This icon lets you manage personal information on three tabs (see Figure 2-19). On the Contact tab, you can enter your mail address and other contact details such as your phone number(s). On the Address tab, you can enter your home and business addresses; and on the Personal Info tab, you can enter other relevant (or irrelevant) personal information. Also useful is the option to change your password; it's a good idea to do that from time to time to decrease the risk of someone guessing it.

Figure 2-19. *Use About Me to enter personal information and change your password.*

■ **Tip** When you enter personal information under About Me, don't forget to include your photo. You can use the Cheese program under Favorites to take your own picture using your webcam.

Appearance

If you don't like the default look of UNR, you need the Appearance program on the Preferences menu. Here, you can switch between the different themes that are available by default. Themes are a convenient way of grouping individual changes to visual elements, such as colors, window borders, and icons. Figure 2-20 shows the interface from which you can select a desktop theme.

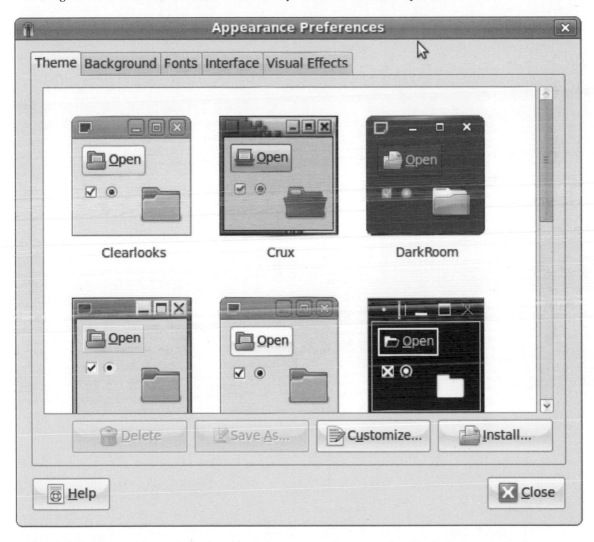

Figure 2-20. You can easily change the appearance of your Ubuntu netbook interface by selecting a different desktop theme.

If you want to change the appearance of your computer's desktop interface, look at the options on the Visual Effects tab. It provides three profiles. The default profile doesn't apply any visual effects. Given the limited capabilities of graphics cards in netbook computers, this isn't a bad idea. But if you want your computer to look better, you can select the Normal visual effects or the Extra option. Be aware that for the latter to work, you need a graphics chip that has 3D support; many Netbooks have that, but there is no guarantee that yours does.

Display

By default, Ubuntu detects your graphics card and screen size. In some cases, however, it starts with the incorrect resolution because something goes wrong in the detection phase. In addition, when your netbook is connected to an external monitor, you must configure what monitor type is used (or connect the monitor and reboot so that Ubuntu detects it automatically).

To configure the external monitor yourself, you work from the Display Preferences window (see Figure 2-21). The easiest way to start is to select the correct resolution from the drop-down list. If the quality of the image still isn't good enough, you can specify the refresh rate to be used. You can even indicate how the display should be rotated by default—for instance, to show the image upside-down, choose Rotation ➤ Upside Down. If you have to connect to external monitors or projectors often, the Show Displays in Panel option is useful. It adds a small icon for instant access to the display properties at upper-right on your screen. When you're finished, click Apply to save your new settings and apply them immediately.

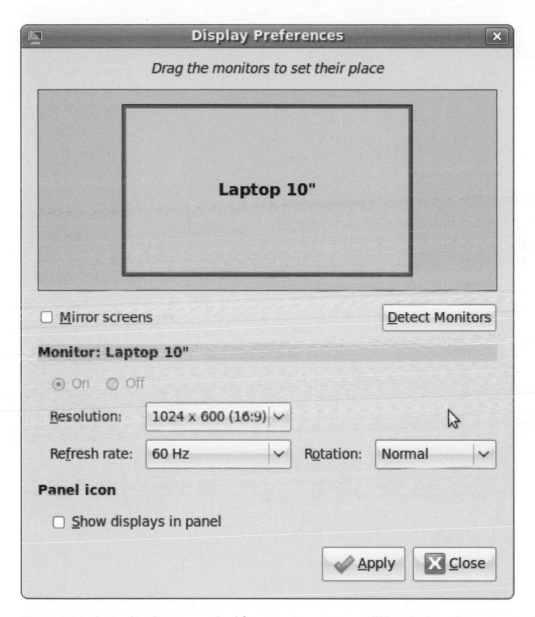

Figure 2-21. *If you often have to work with external monitors, you'll benefit from the options in the Display Preferences application.*

Main Menu

A most interesting option is offered by the Main Menu application on the Preferences tab. This application allows you to change what you see by default in the netbook launcher interface. After opening this application, you'll recognize the default menu options that are shown when you start UNR (see Figure 2-22). As you can see, other menu options are available as well; in some cases, it may be worth considering changing some of the default settings. For instance, not everyone needs the Universal Access items, but some people will appreciate the options presented under System Tools or Other. If this is the case for you, select and deselect what you want to work with.

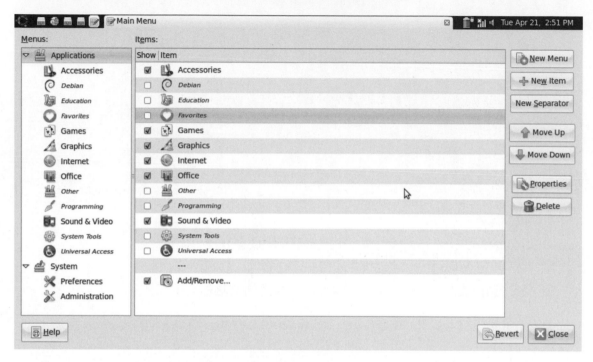

Figure 2-22. You can tune the main menu of the interface to your own needs.

■ **Tip** In some cases, you'll encounter windows that are larger than your netbook's screen. To handle them, press the Alt key and click and drag anywhere on the window to move it around. Or press Alt-F7 and move the window with the arrow keys, anchoring it with a mouse click when it's in the desired position.

In some cases, you'll also need to add new items to the Main Menu. Imagine that you've just installed your favorite application, but no default menu item is created for it. The following procedure describes how you can add a menu item for this new application. I'll use Skype as the example (in Chapter 6, you'll learn how to install this application):

1. You need to find the exact location where the application file is located. To do so, open a terminal window from the Accessories menu item; then, in that window, type whereis skype. The command will show you that it has found a program file with the name /usr/bin/skype. That's the name you need, so be sure you remember it (or select it and choose Edit ➤ Copy in Terminal so you can paste it later).

2. Go to the Main Menu editor, and click New Item. Doing so opens the interface shown in Figure 2-23.

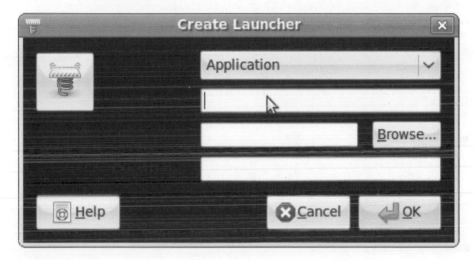

Figure 2-23. From the Create Launcher interface, you can add new items to the main menu.

3. Enter the type of item you're adding. It will be an application in most cases. Then, type the name of the application (or paste it, if you copied it earlier) and the exact location where you can find it, with an optional description, and click OK to apply and save changes. This adds the new application to the menu item that's currently selected.

Screensaver

From time to time, you'll take a moment off and do nothing with your netbook. At those moments, your netbook can activate a screensaver. By default, this happens after 10 minutes of inactivity, and the screen goes black. Some other options are available as well.

If you wish, you can select a fancy screensaver. One of my personal favorites is the Cosmos screensaver, which gives you a relaxing view of the galaxy. You may also like the F-Spot screensaver, which shows you the photos you've imported into the F-Spot photo-management utility (see Chapter 6 for more details). Try all of them—after clicking a screensaver, you immediately see what it looks like in the example window (see Figure 2-24).

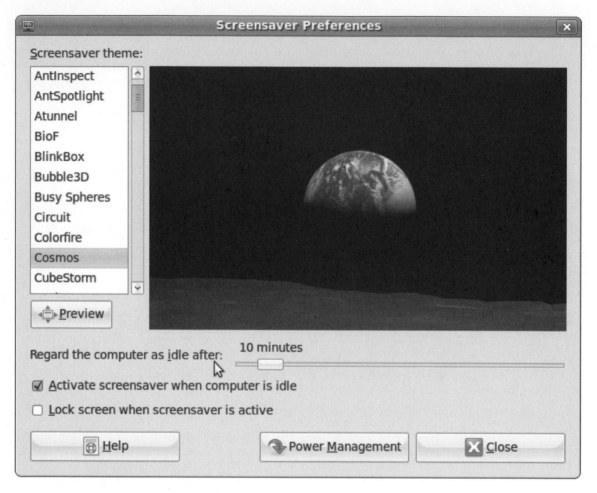

Figure 2-24. Click the available screensavers to see what they look like.

From the Screensaver Preferences interface, you can also select the option to lock the screen when the screensaver is active. When using this option, you need to enter the password of the current user before you can access the desktop again.

■ **Tip** You can add an applet to the panel (the upper-left part of your screen) to lock screen access in one click. Right-click the panel to open a menu that includes the Add to Panel option. Select this option, and click the Lock Screen applet. This adds an icon of a computer monitor with a lock next to it. Click it to lock your computer monitor if you go away for a while. Alternatively, memorize the keyboard shortcut Ctrl-Alt-L, which does the same trick.

Switch Desktop Mode

The last option from the Preferences menu that I'll discuss here is the Switch Desktop Mode application. Using this application, you can switch between the netbook launcher interface and the classic Ubuntu desktop (see Figure 2-25).

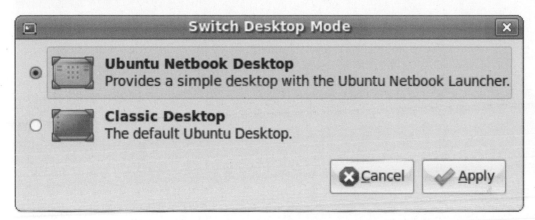

Figure 2-25. The Switch Desktop Mode application allows you to switch between the classic Ubuntu desktop and the Ubuntu netbook desktop.

If you're used to the classic Ubuntu desktop (the one you see when working with Ubuntu on a normal-size computer), you may want to choose the Classic Desktop look using this application. It shows you the normal Ubuntu desktop (see Figure 2-26). All the applications you use in the Ubuntu netbook layout are still there, but the way the desktop is organized has completely changed.

Figure 2-26. *The classic Ubuntu desktop look allows you to work with the same Ubuntu interface that you may know from a normal installation.*

In this book, I'll only use the Ubuntu netbook interface. So, if you want to switch back at this point, feel free to do so. You can switch back by selecting System ➤ Preferences ➤ Switch Desktop Mode. Then, select Ubuntu Netbook Desktop.

Quitting

If your hardware is completely supported, you can close the cover of your netbook computer to suspend it. While it's suspended, it uses very little power. Unfortunately, not all netbooks support this feature yet. Hence, you'll probably need the Quit menu option located in the lower-right corner of the netbook launcher interface, which brings up a set of logout and shutdown options (see Figure 2-27). These options are summarized here:

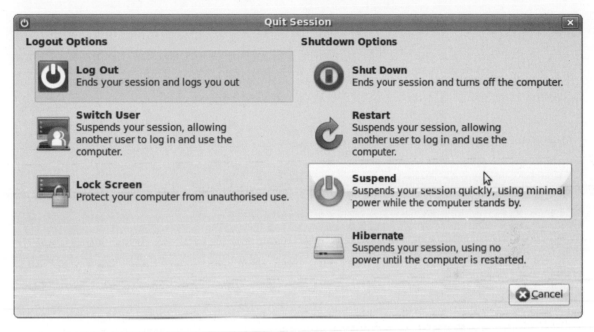

Figure 2-27. Use the Quit menu option to access all the available options to terminate your session.

- *Log Out*: This ends your current session. To establish a new session, you need to enter your user name and password.

- *Switch User*: This option is useful if you're on a computer where different user accounts exist. By using this option, your current settings and all the programs you have open are saved, and another user can log in and do some work. When the other user has finished, you can use Switch User again to return to your account settings.

- *Lock Screen*: Use this option to lock access to the screen if you go away from your computer. Access is allowed only after you enter your password.

- *Shut Down*: This option ends your computer session and turns off the computer. Use this if you want to use no battery power and you aren't planning to start using the computer again soon.

- *Restart*: This option restarts your computer. You're disconnected, and all services and active programs are terminated. After the netbook restarts, you can log on again and start all the programs you need.

- *Suspend*: Using this option, you suspend your sessions and save your current working environment to memory. This option uses some power while suspended and offers the benefit that you can return to your working environment quickly.

- *Hibernate*: This option saves your current session to disk and closes down the computer. The netbook uses no power while in hibernation, but it will take more time to begin working again. To restart the computer from either suspend or hibernate mode, push the power button briefly.

Summary

In this chapter, you've learned how to find your way around on a netbook computer that has the UNR installed. You've learned where to find your programs, how to work with files, and how to change some of the settings related to the appearance of your netbook computer. In the next chapter, you'll learn how to get connected and use the most important Internet applications.

CHAPTER 3

■ ■ ■

Getting Connected

What is the point of a netbook? The Net, of course! Among the most important aspects of netbook computers is how easy they make it to get connected, anywhere. In this chapter, you'll learn how to connect. The following topics are covered:

- Configuring Bluetooth
- Connecting to a 3G network
- Connecting to a wired network
- Connecting to a wireless network

Configuring Bluetooth

No matter how you connect your computer to the Internet, it may be necessary to use Bluetooth, especially if you want to connect your cell phone to your computer. So before I start talking about the way you connect your computer to the Internet using 3G on your cell phone, I'll talk about Bluetooth configuration.

You can tell that your computer has Bluetooth if a Bluetooth icon appears in the panel at the top of the screen. If it doesn't, from the Preferences menu, open the Bluetooth item to access the available Bluetooth options (see Figure 3-1).

■ **Note** Some brands of netbook manufacturers don't have an internal Bluetooth adapter. For instance, the popular Acer Aspire One lacks this feature. If you haven't yet bought a netbook computer, make sure the one you buy has Bluetooth—it's a very convenient feature.

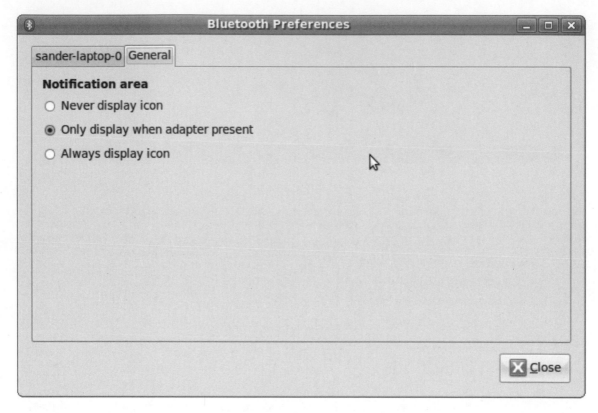

Figure 3-1. Use the Bluetooth icon to set up Bluetooth connection options.

The Bluetooth Preferences item offers two tabs with configuration options. First, you can specify when the Bluetooth icon should appear. The default setting displays the icon in the panel only when a Bluetooth adapter is present. You should probably keep it that way, because it offers the most convenient means of setting up a Bluetooth connection and it makes sense not to show the icon if no Bluetooth adapter is present. If for any reason you prefer not to use this option, select Never Display Icon if you never want to see the Bluetooth connection menu, or Always Display Icon if you always want to see it, regardless of whether an adapter is present.

After you specify whether you want to see the connection icon, you can specify visibility settings on your computer's configuration tab. In this window, you can configure two items. First is the visibility of your netbook computer. Others people who want to establish a link to your computer need to be able to see your computer before they can access it. If you want to exchange files with someone else, and the other person asks how to connect to your computer, you may choose to make your computer visible.

Be aware that Bluetooth visibility imposes a security risk; if your netbook is visible, anyone can try to make a connection to your computer—and you probably don't want that. If you need to make your computer visible so that others can connect to it, I recommend using the Temporary Visible option so you don't forget to turn visibility off again. When you do this, you can also specify how long you want your computer to be visible. Figure 3-2 shows the slide bar you use to define the amount of time your computer should be visible. The default value of 3 minutes is normally a good suggestion; 3 minutes should be long enough for others to connect to your computer.

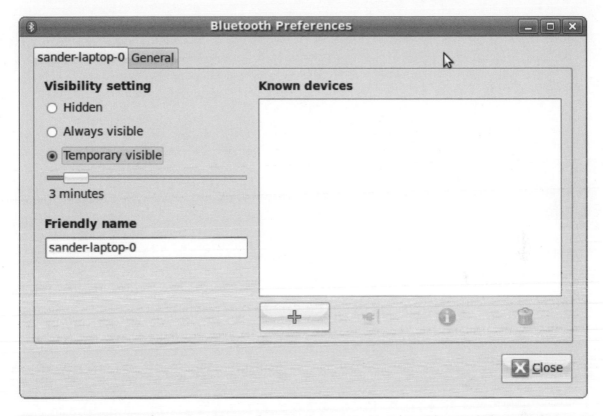

Figure 3-2. *If others need to make a Bluetooth connection to your computer, it's a good idea to make it visible only temporarily.*

To make a connection to your mobile phone so that you can use it as a modem to get on the Internet, you don't need the Visibility setting. Just click the + sign in the Bluetooth Preferences window to add the new Bluetooth connection. Doing so starts the Bluetooth Device Wizard, which in its first step shows a welcome message. In this window, click Forward to proceed.

Your neighborhood is now checked for available devices. Several devices may appear; if this is the case, make sure you wait until scanning for devices is complete. When it is, you should recognize the correct device by its name (see Figure 3-3).

Figure 3-3. After scanning, select the device you want to connect to.

Now, select the device. Use the Automatic PIN Code Selection option; it generates a PIN code for you automatically, which you need to use on the device to initiate the connection. When this PIN code is displayed, click Forward. At this point, you should see a message on your cell phone, indicating that your computer wants to establish a connection. Accept this request, and enter the PIN code that was generated by your netbook. Doing so initiates the connection (see Figure 3-4).

Figure 3-4. After you accept the incoming connection and enter the PIN code, your Bluetooth connection is established.

Connecting to a 3G network

Imagine that you want to be able to connect no matter you are. In that case, using a 3G network is probably your best option. 3G works over virtually any cell phone network, so the setup requirements are minimal.

There are different ways to connect to a 3G network. The easiest way is to use the 3G available on many modern cell phones. You'll read about configuring this in the next section. Another method is to connect a 3G USB dongle to your netbook. When you do this, the configuration is similar to the configuration with a mobile phone.

Connecting Your Netbook to a Cell Phone

Before you can dial in to the Internet, you need to connect your netbook to your cell phone. Basically, you have two options: using USB or using Bluetooth. If you're using a USB cable, connect your cell phone to the netbook with that cable. Your computer will automatically detect the new connection type. Connecting by USB is the easiest method—no additional setup is required—but it may not be the most convenient setup method, because you need to carry an additional cable. Hence, if your netbook has Bluetooth, it's a better option.

   If your computer doesn't have an internal Bluetooth interface, it isn't the end of the world. Just connect an external Bluetooth adapter, and it will pick up the Bluetooth connection automatically.

Using Your Cell Phone as a Modem

If you've connected your computer to your cell phone, you can use it to dial in to the Internet. To do this, right-click the Internet connection icon in the toolbar, and select the Edit Connections option from the menu (see Figure 3-5).

Figure 3-5. *Select Edit Connections to create a new connection.*

   The Network Connections window offers different options to establish a network connection, depending on the type of connection you need. Because you're trying to initialize a mobile broadband connection, choose the Mobile Broadband tab and then click Add to set up the Internet connection using your cell phone (see Figure 3-6).

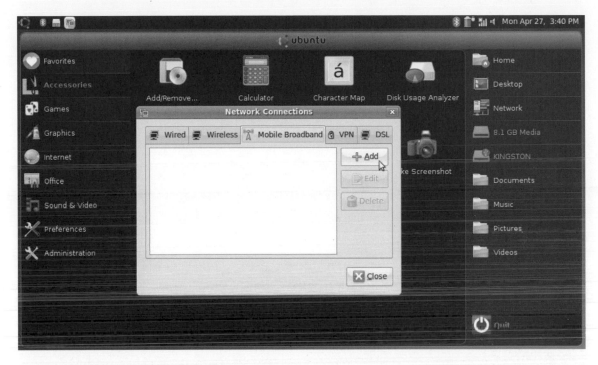

Figure 3-6. You can create the 3G network connection using the Mobile Broadband tab.

The New Mobile Broadband Connection Wizard opens. This wizard shows you its welcome message; click Forward to proceed. In the next step, enter the connection details for your service provider. First, select your country; next, select your provider from the list of available providers (see Figure 3-7). Then, click Forward to proceed.

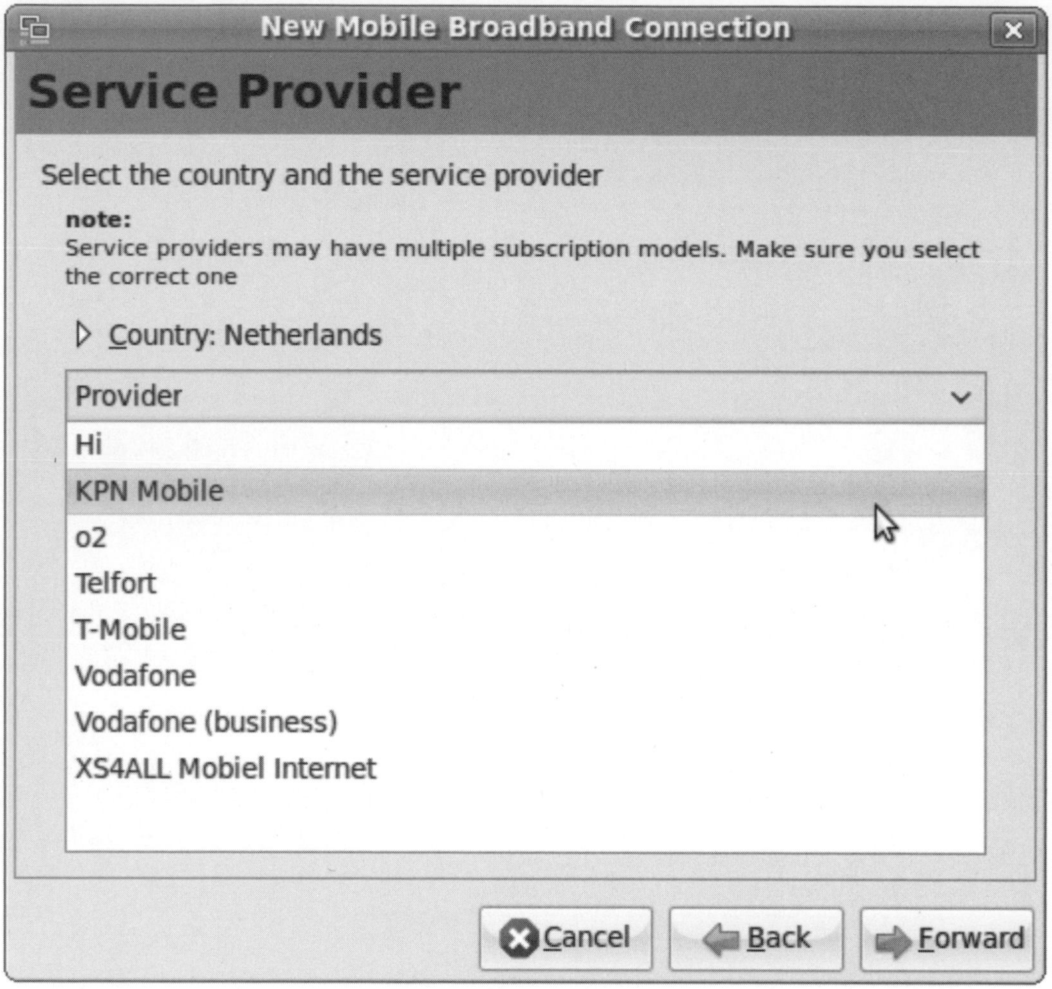

Figure 3-7. First select your country, and next select the provider for your 3G connection.

In the Summary screen that appears (see Figure 3-8), you see the country and provider you selected. You also have the option to enter a name for this connection. If everything is correct, click Apply to save your changes.

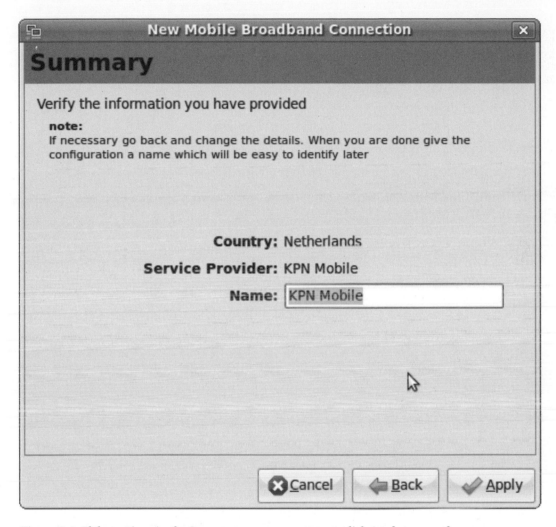

Figure 3-8. If the settings in the Summary screen are correct, click Apply to save them.

Your cell phone is ready for use as a modem. Right-click the network connection icon, and select the new connection type. You can now start working on the Internet.

Connecting to a Wireless Network

Another way to get connected is to use a wireless network. A wireless network typically is fixed around an access point, which is referred to as a *hot spot* if it's in a public place, but you can also your own wireless network at home. This access point is connected to a wired network that often offers high-speed access to the Internet.

Wireless networks are owned by someone. You'll find them in many public places, like airports and hotels. Some wireless network owners charges you a fee to connect, and others don't. In exchange for the access fee, you often get a connection that is decent and performs well. But many people have a wireless network at home, which makes using your netbook very convenient. Netbooks are great for a surfing on the sofa or looking up recipes on the Internet in the kitchen.

In addition, if you travel a lot, wireless networks are the way to get connected. Cheap Internet access using 3G networks often stops at the borders of your country; while you're traveling, 3G network access may become (extremely) expensive. Wireless, on the other hand, is often available for free; and if it isn't, you at least know that you can keep the cost under control.

Wireless Networking Background

When you connect to a wireless network, you need to know something about its background. First, there are commonly two types of wireless networks: networks with and networks without security. This security is normally enforced using encryption. With encryption, the data you send (including passwords) is scrambled before it's sent over the air, which makes it impossible for other people to intercept what you're sending. You should try to always use encryption when you connect to a wireless network.

You'll find unsecured wireless networks in some private environments and badly protected public places. You should avoid them, because other people can read the data you're transmitting. This means there's a chance that bad people are present and sniffing the network to see if any interesting data passes by—for example, wireless users' credit-card numbers and personal passwords.

Wireless security is usually based on a password (also known as the *encryption key*), so you need to know the password to get connected. This isn't always practical in a public place—what's the use of a password if anyone can call the front desk of your hotel to ask for it? Nevertheless, a bad password is better than no password at all. A password requirement is more common in private places. There are different kinds of passwords that need to be entered; some are defined in the Wired Equivalent Privacy (WEP) protocol, and others are defined in the Wi-Fi Protected Access (WPA) protocol.

■ **Note** WEP is old-school encryption for wireless networks, and it can easily be cracked. However, it gives some amount of protection, so use it if nothing else is offered. If possible, it's much better to use another form of encryption. Currently, WPA2 is the most secure and most popular method to protect your wireless network.

When you're setting up a connection, you need to know which password type the wireless network of your choice is using. The owner of the network can provide this information. Before you start, make sure you have the answers to the following questions. If you do, you can proceed with the next section:

- Does your wireless network require you to enter a password (key) or anything like that?

- If so, what is the password?

- Does the wireless network use the WEP or the WPA protocol?

You may encounter cases where you have to authenticate at some other level. For example, the wireless network itself may be open, but you have to authenticate to a proxy server that enables your Internet connection. This method is used quite often in paid wireless networks, such as those in hotels, airport lounges, and other public places. You should be aware that such a network offers no protection whatsoever (so your data may be intercepted by someone else). These public wireless networks only have you authenticate on the proxy so they can make you pay for using the Internet connection.

Connecting to the Wireless Network

To connect to the wireless network, begin by clicking the network connection icon in the toolbar. If the wireless network isn't hidden, you'll probably see it listed (see listing 3-9). Select it.

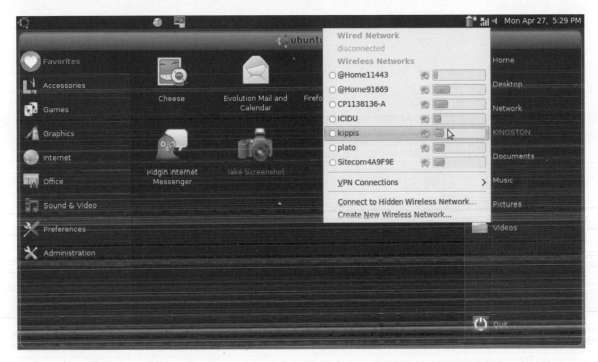

Figure 3-9. If the wireless network of your choice isn't hidden, select it to make a connection.

If the network of your choice is protected, you're prompted to enter a key or a password. The exact options that are available depend on the network you're connecting to; hence, you may not see all the options listed in this section when connecting to a particular network. You can find different security options in the drop-down menu at the Wireless Security option, which opens automatically if authentication is required (see Figure 3-10).

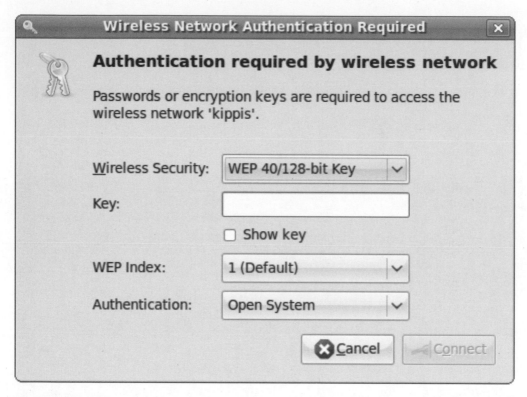

Figure 3-10. The Wireless Security option that appears depends on the kind of security the wireless network of your choice is using.

■ **Note** In most cases, Ubuntu determines what kind of security is used on your wireless network and automatically offers the options that are relevant for that security configuration. In some cases—especially if a less common security setting is used—it may offer you the wrong option. In that case, you must enter the required information.

If the settings for your wireless network aren't detected automatically, you can specify them yourself. The following security options are available:

- *WPA & WPA2 Personal*: This option comes up automatically if the wireless network of your choice uses WPA for its security. In this case, you need to enter a password to connect.

- *WEP 40/128-bit Key*: This is the classic protection used for wireless networks. You'll probably need to select this if your password (the key) consists of numbers and letters *A–F* only.

- *WEP 128-bit Passphrase*: Use this option if you've obtained a real password.

- *LEAP*: LEAP is a very specific protocol. You'll find it in business networks that use Cisco hardware to establish network connections. Try this option if neither WEP 40/128-bit Key nor WEP 128-bit Passphrase works.

- *Dynamic WEP (802.1x):* This solution also isn't used often. You'll find it in some business networks. Try it if none of the other options work out well.

Depending on the option you select for security, you may see some other options as well. For instance, if you select WEP as the authentication option, you need to specify the authentication type. You can choose between Open System and Shared Key authentication; in almost all cases, you need the Shared Key authentication option, where you enter a secret key that the administrator of the wireless network gives you. A WEP network may use more than one WEP key. If this is the case, you may need to specify which WEP index you're on, to ensure that you're using the correct authentication credentials. The Shared Key authentication option is used when the administrator of the network configures different WEP keys, which is sometimes done to differentiate between groups of users. In any case, WEP is getting increasingly rare these days, because WPA security is much better and supported as good as WEP.

Connecting to an Unlisted Wireless Network

If the wireless network of your choice is in the list of available networks, connecting is easy: select the network, and enter your authentication credentials. If it's not, there are two options to make the connection manually:

- *Connect to Hidden Wireless Network*: Use this option if the administrator has deliberately hidden the wireless network you want to connect to.

- *Create New Wireless Network*: Choose this if for any other reason that isn't completely clear, you can't connect to your wireless network.

You can find both of these options at the bottom of the menu you see after clicking the network connection icon in the toolbar.

Connecting to a Hidden Wireless Network

One way to secure a wireless network is to hide it. This form of security is old school and not very effective, because nowadays many tools exist to find a hidden wireless network. Nevertheless, if the administrator of your wireless network has hidden the network, you can set up a connection by adding the wireless network by hand. The following procedure describes how to do that:

1. Click the network access icon on your computer's toolbar. Select Connect to Hidden Wireless Network from the menu. This opens the window shown in Figure 3-11.

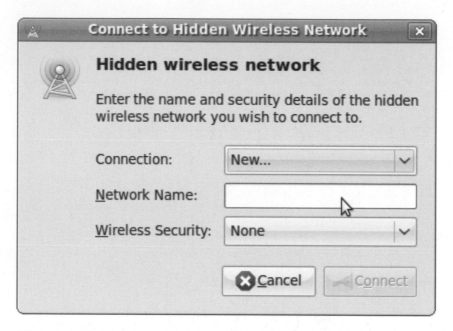

Figure 3-11. Enter the network name and security option to configure access to a hidden wireless network.

2. Select the New Connection option. Next, enter the name of the wireless network (ask the administrator) and the type of wireless security the network is using.

3. Click Connect to automatically connect to the wireless network.

Creating a New Wireless Connection

If for some reason, the options just described don't work, you can add a new wireless connection. To do this, click the network connection icon on the toolbar, and select Create New Wireless Network from the menu. Next, in the window shown in Figure 3-12, enter the name of the network and the wireless security mode you want to use, and click Create. You're immediately connected to the wireless network you just created.

Figure 3-12. If nothing else works, you can create your own wireless connection.

Troubleshooting Wireless Connections

Normally, at this point you should be connected. If you aren't, some limited options are available for troubleshooting. The best method for troubleshooting is to remove your connection and create it again. As an alternative, you can try to modify the properties of the wireless connection. I recommend that you do that only if removing and adding the connection again doesn't work.

The following procedure describes how to delete a connection, after which you can use the procedure from the previous section to create the connection again:

1. Right-click the network connection icon on your computer's toolbar. From the menu that pops up, select Edit Connections.

2. In the Network Connections window, select the Wireless tab (see Figure 3-13). This brings up a list of all the wireless networks you've ever selected.

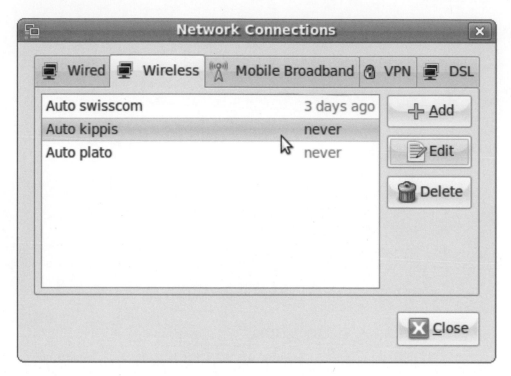

Figure 3-13. On the Wireless tab, you have access to all wireless networks you've ever accessed.

3. Select the wireless network you're having problems with, and click Delete to remove it from the list. All the configuration used in the past is removed, and you can try connecting again.

Connecting to a Wired Network

Most network connections today are wireless. Nevertheless, if you want the best possible performance and reliability, it's always better to take a network cable and connect your netbook to a wired network. Let there be no misunderstanding about the cables. You can't use just any cable—you need to connect a specific unshielded twisted pair (UTP) network cable to the RJ-45 socket on your netbook. Not sure what kind of cable that is? No problem; Figure 3-14 shows you exactly what you need.

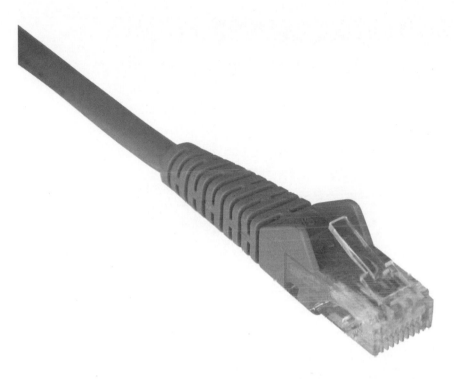

Figure 3-14. *You need this type of network cable to connect to a wired network.*

After you connect, normally no additional configuration is required. Wired network connections are plug-and-play most of the time. That is, you plug the network cable into your netbook computer, you automatically receive all the configuration required to connect to the network, and you can start using the Internet. But sometimes it's useful to find out the properties of the network connection you're using. To check, right-click the network connection icon (which now looks like two small computer screens instead of the vertical bars you see for a wireless connection). From the menu, select Connection Information. This brings up the screen shown in Figure 3-15.

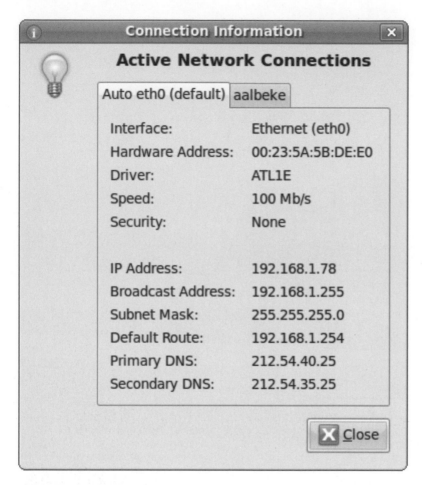

Figure 3-15. Using the Connection Information menu option, you can see all properties your network connection currently is using.

For you, this configuration may mean nothing. But for a network expert who is trying to help you get your network connection up and running, this is useful information indeed. It shows all the addresses you're using to connect to the network, which is very helpful if you're having trouble connecting. Make sure you know where to find this information if you need it.

Analyzing and Troubleshooting Network Connections

You should now be happily connected to the Internet and doing whatever you want with your netbook computer. In some cases, however, it doesn't work out the way you want, and you need to do more to get connected. That's what this section is about. First, you'll learn how to use the Network Tools to analyze what is happening on your network connection. Next, you'll learn how to use advanced network properties to connect if the default options don't work.

■ **Note** The information in this section won't be of interest to all readers. But if you want to be able to troubleshoot your network connection, no matter what kind of connection that is, you'll find the tools mentioned here useful.

Analyzing Network Connections Using the Network Tools

In some cases, you need to go beyond displaying the properties of a network interface and test if it works. To do so, you use the Network Tools option on the Administration menu. This is a collection of eight tools, all of them useful.

Devices

When you start the Network Tools, you see the Devices tab. On this tab, you get access to the properties of your network card. Beware: by default, the Loopback device is selected, and that's probably not what you want. Click the drop-down list by the Network Device option to show a list of all devices that are available at the moment (see Figure 3-16); those that aren't available are grayed out in the menu. Select the device for which you want to see statistics.

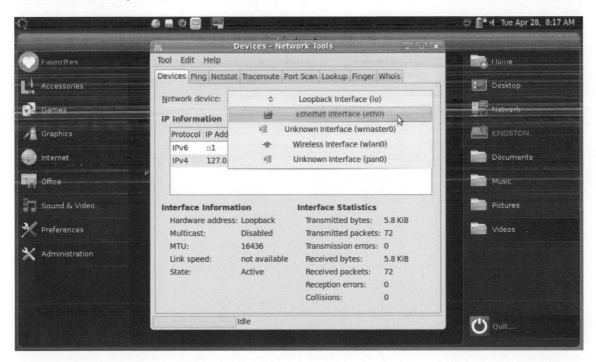

Figure 3-16. Select the device for which you want to see statistics.

The most important information about the network device is the IP address. A network card needs an IP address to connect to other computers. In most cases, this address is assigned automatically. If for some reason you don't see an IP address, you should ask the person who is responsible for the network what is wrong. The network interface's State should be Active; and in the Interface Statistics section, the network card should show some transmitted bytes as well as received bytes. On a network card that has already been up for a long time, you should see multiple megabytes here; the interface for which you see statistics in Figure 3-17 has only just been activated.

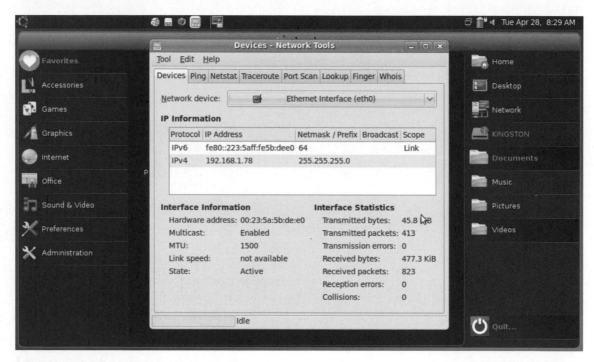

Figure 3-17. A network card that has been active for a long time should show more than just a few transmitted and received bytes.

Ping

After you determine that your network card does have an IP address, you need to test whether it's able to talk to other computers. You do this from the Ping tab. On this tab, you're asked to enter a network address. You can use an address (137.65.1.1 has never failed me under normal operational circumstanced) or a domain name (www.sander.fr, for instance). Enter the name of the computer for which you want to test connectivity (see Figure 3-18), and specify how many requests you want to send. To test connectivity on your local desktop computer, there is no reason to go beyond the default 5 packets. Next, click Ping to start your connectivity test. If all goes well, it shows you that the number of succesful packets is 100%. If you see anything below 80%, you may be testing on a very busy or a very remote computer. If you can, find a computer closer to you.

Another useful part of the ping utility is the response time. A normal response time is measured in tenths of milliseconds. So, if you're getting something like a 20 ms response time, that is good, and you can use applications that need a fast Internet connection (IP telephone, for instance) without too much trouble. If the response time is greater than about 100 ms, the connection isn't fast enough for time-sensitive applications. In certain situations, ping helps you find out why a given application isn't working the way you expect.

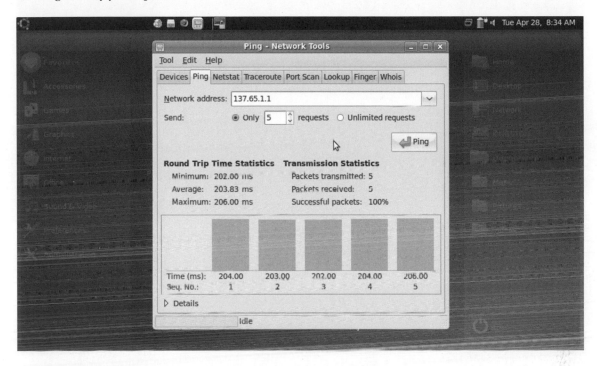

Figure 3-18. Use ping to test whether and how quickly you can reach other computers.

Netstat

The Netstat utility gives you information about networking on your computer. Two pieces of the information it provides are interesting. First, Netstat can show you routing table information. In its *routing table*, a computer keeps the information it needs to communicate with computers on other networks. The routing table should at least show you a default route: 0.0.0.0. If it doesn't, the person who's responsible for your network has made an error. In Figure 3-19, you can see that this default route is defined and that it uses the computer with address 192.168.1.254 as the default gateway. (It's a good idea to test that address next, because if the default gateway isn't working, you can't go anywhere.)

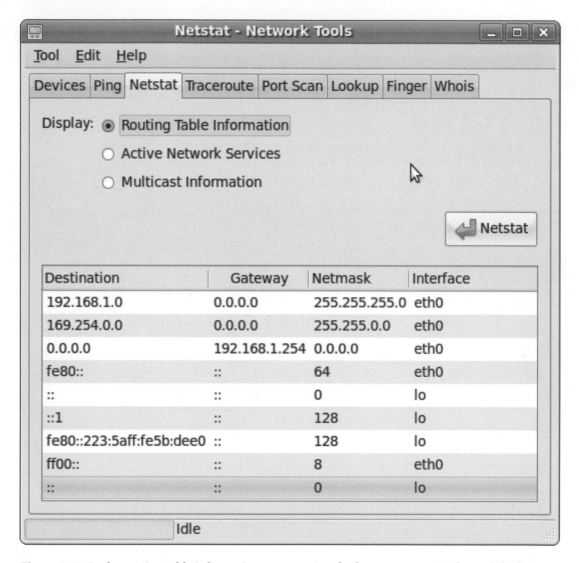

Figure 3-19. In the routing table information, you can see whether your computer has a default route.

If your computer is providing services to other computers, it's interesting to see if these services are available. This information can also help you find out whether someone has made an unauthorized connection to your computer. Normally, on the Netstat tab, the Active Network Services list should be very short. In the example in listing 3-20, port 631 is listening. No worries—this is the print server. Some other ports that are connected to applications are available as well; but there's nothing to worry about here. If you see a line that has the state CONNECTED, you should start worrying. In that case, someone has an open connection to your computer and may be doing nasty things. But because your Ubuntu system has a firewall activated by default, you should see no problems.

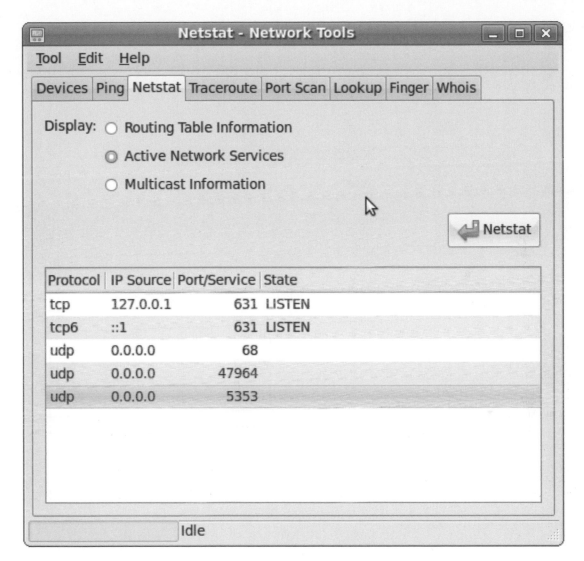

Figure 3-20. In the list of active services, you shouldn't see much more than the print server that is listening to incoming connections.

Traceroute

You probably won't work with the Traceroute utility much. This tool lists all routers that were needed to connect to the remote computer you're testing connectivity with. This lets you see exactly how packets are sent over the Internet and what routers are used to do that. Normally, this utility gives you a list of computer addresses and names that make sense to experts only. But if you're interested, it shows you part of the world-wide travel your packets often make. For instance, Figure 3-21 shows that packets were sent through a router in Amsterdam (AMS) and ultimately went through Chicago (ORD) to arrive in Dallas (DFW), where they continued on their way.

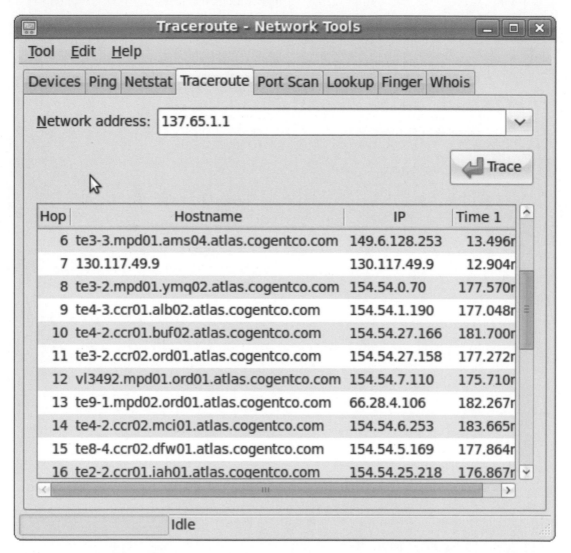

Figure 3-21. The Traceroute tool shows you how packets travel over the Internet to reach their final destination.

■ **Note** Routers on the Internet often have airport codes included in their names. Based on the airport code, you know the location of the router you're connecting to.

Port Scan

Let me make this clear: you should *never* use Port Scan against computers that you don't own or random computers on the Internet. Scanning ports is considered a hostile act by most network providers—that is, an attack against their computers. The least that will happen to you is that you're likely to be disconnected from their network. But if you're scanning ports on computers you own, you may get some useful information.

By scanning ports, you can analyze which services the target computer provides. This information may be useful if, for instance, you need to find out whether the web server you're running in your home network is operational. But scanning ports requires administrative skills as well. If you don't know the difference between WWW and SSH, don't even bother using Port Scan. If you do know the difference, Port Scan provides a useful tool to get an overview of services that are provided by any computer in the network. For instance, you can use it to check whether popular services are available on any network node (see Figure 3-22). Some of these include port 25 (**Simple Mail Transfer Protocol** [SMTP]), which should be present on most mail servers; port 80, which you may expect to be open on a web server; and port 22, which should be offered on a machine you want to connect to for a remote terminal session using the Secure Shell (SSH) program.

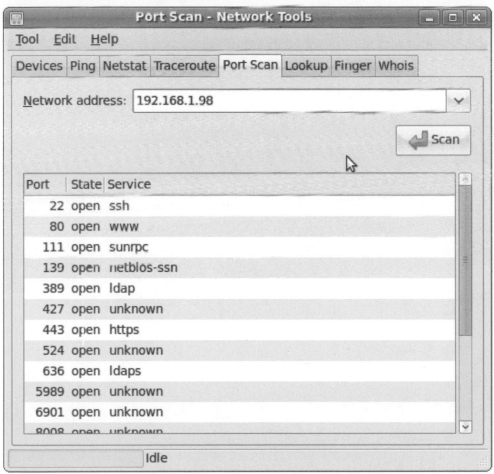

Figure 3-22. The Port Scan utility gives a list of services that are provided by a computer in your network.

Lookup

The Lookup utility gives you an overview of known information about a target computer. Most of this information is related to the Domain Name System (DNS) information. One responsibility of DNS is to provide names for servers on the Internet. If you can't reach any server by its name, but only by its address, it may be useful to test DNS by using the options on the Lookup tab. In the Network Address field, enter the name of the server you want to test; then, click Lookup. It returns a list like the one in Figure 3-23. In this list, you can see that a couple of DNS name servers are responsible for translating the address of this target server to a name (summarized in the three lines that have the NS record type). If this list stays empty, you should notify the person responsible for the network that something is wrong with their DNS servers. After changing a setting on the server, they can then make sure you get connected again. Or perhaps your network setup is wrong, and as a result, you can't use DNS.

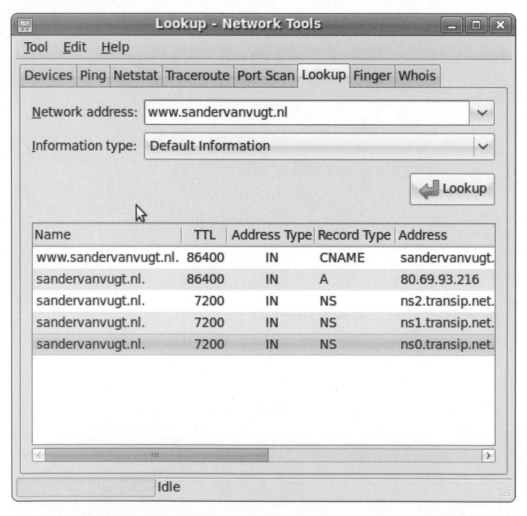

Figure 3-23. The Lookup tool allows you to check if the DNS server you're using is operational.

Finger

Finger is an old tool, and for security reasons, it's disabled in most cases. If enabled, it shows you information about the activity of a user on a given computer. If this tool gives you a result on a computer, that means something is seriously wrong with that computer's security settings. Just ignore Finger—it doesn't provide anything useful in most cases.

Whois

Whois is an advanced tool. It gives you information about the person who owns a certain name on the Internet. Try it on any name on the Internet: you'll be surprised how much privacy-related information is displayed on some occasions (see Figure 3-24)!

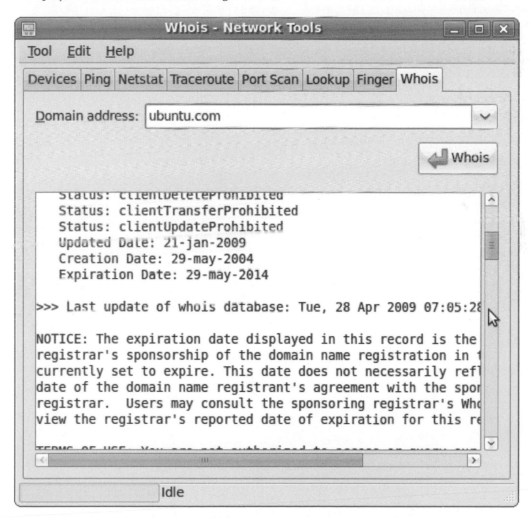

Figure 3-24. The Whois tool can show you who owns a name on the Internet.

Editing Advanced Network Properties

In some cases, your network may need specific information to connect. In most situations, it's good enough if you automatically get an address to connect to the network (the so-called IP address) when connecting. But in other situations, this won't do. When that happens, you can edit many properties of the network connection by hand. Some of these are for network specialists only; but to be complete, this section provides an overview of all the available settings.

To access the settings for your network card, right-click the network connection icon, and select Edit Connections. This brings you to the Network Connections interface. In this window, activate the tab that has the network connection you want to edit. For example, say it's a wireless connection; you click the Wireless tab. This gives you a list of all the wireless networks that you've connected to in the past. To access the properties of such a connection, click it, and then click the Edit button.

This opens the interface where you can modify properties of the selected connection. For a wireless connection, the window has three tabs. The first tab displays the properties of the wireless network you're connecting with (see Figure 3-25). Make sure the name of the wireless network is in the SSID field and Mode is set to Infrastructure (this should be set automatically) Also select the Connect Automatically option, which automatically enables this connection when your computer starts. The other parameters on this tab are rarely used.

Figure 3-25. To make a connection with a wireless network, be sure you have an SSID and Infrastructure connection mode.

The Wireless Security tab (see Figure 3-26) gives you access to the security options you entered when establishing the connection. You need to enter the correct security type and the password to access the network. Be sure you use the correct security settings, because they aren't always detected the right way.

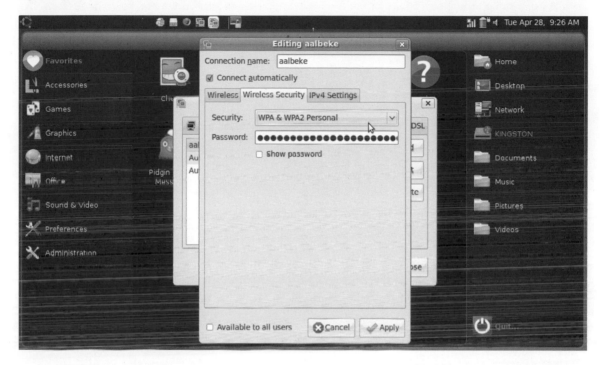

Figure 3-26. Be sure you select the correct security settings.

The last tab displays Internet Protocol version 4 (IPv4) settings. IPv4 is the protocol that gives your computer an address to connect to the network; and at the very least, you need an address to get connected. The default method used to obtain an IPv4 address is Shared to Other Computers. That means your computer gets an IP address automatically and this IP address isn't exclusively reserved for your computer. If that poses a problem, you can change this option to Automatic (DHCP), which ensures that your computer automatically gets an IP address and also that it tries to get the same IP address all the time (see Figure 3-27).

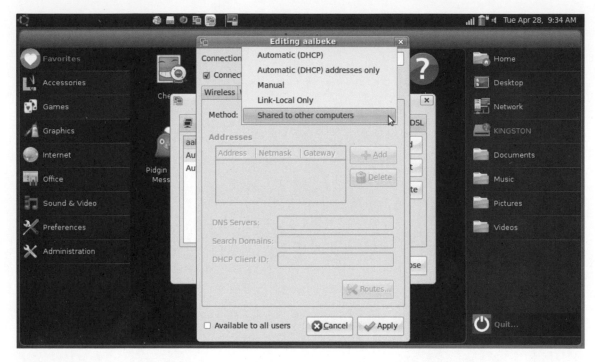

Figure 3-27. *There are different ways to get an address that will let you access the network.*

If these methods to get an IP address don't work, you can add the network configuration by hand. In that case, you need to ask the person responsible for the network for the appropriate connection details. To enter these, on the IPv4 settings tab, set Method to Manual, and then click Add to enter the IP address configuration. You must now enter the IP address, the network, and the gateway. Next, in the DNS Servers field, enter the IP address of a DNS server. Does this sound like Greenlandic to you? If so, ask the person who is responsible for the network you're connecting with—they can provide all the necessary details. After you entering this information, the interface looks like Figure 3-28. Click Apply to save and activate this configuration.

Figure 3-28. *If no server is handing out IP addresses automatically, you need to enter the required information yourself.*

Summary

In this chapter, you've learned how to connect to the Internet with your netbook. You can use many methods to do this. First, you can use Bluetooth on the netbook to connect to an external device (although using a USB cable to connect to that device may easier). Next, you learned how to connect to a wireless network. The last part of this chapter explained how to configure the network interface on your netbook with a fixed IP address configuration. In the next chapter, you'll find out what to do with your netbook after you're connected to the Internet. You'll explore some of the many cool applications you can use to communicate on the Net.

CHAPTER 4

■ ■ ■

Netbook Online

At this point you're connected to the Internet, so you have access to mail, web, chat, IP telephony, and much more. In this chapter, you'll learn how to use all that functionality. The following topics are covered:

- Using the Firefox web browser

- E-mail and calendars in Evolution

- Internet telephony with Skype

- Instant messaging with Pidgin

Using the Firefox Web Browser

You may have already worked with Firefox, the default web browser on Ubuntu Netbook Remix. If you've been using Windows until now, the browser you used was probably Microsoft's Internet Explorer. Firefox has emerged as a successor to the Netscape browser, which was popular until 1995, when Microsoft released Windows 95. In those days, nearly everyone used Windows, and there was a real risk that Microsoft would claim the Internet as well. However, in recent years Firefox has taken a sizeable market share from the Microsoft monopoly.

Firefox is available for the three major platforms: Apple, Linux, and Windows. Even Windows users tend to like Firefox. There are some important reasons: it's fast (much faster than Internet Explorer), and it offers features that were added to Internet Explorer at a much later date. Examples include the use of tabs in the browser, and the way it works with an extensions architecture that lets you add extra features.

Firefox has also played an important role in making the Internet as the way it is today. Because of Firefox, developers can develop web sites using open standards and programming languages that aren't dictated by Microsoft. The popularity of Firefox is still increasing; currently it has more users than ever. If you've never worked with it before, you'll soon find out why it's so popular.

You can find an icon to start the Firefox web browser in the Favorites menu. In addition, an icon on the Internet menu groups together all Internet-related applications that are installed by default. After you start Firefox, it brings you to the Ubuntu welcome page, which is a file stored on the local hard disk of your computer (see Figure 4-1). As you are probably well aware, to go to another web site, just enter the address in the address bar and press Enter (see Figure 4-2).

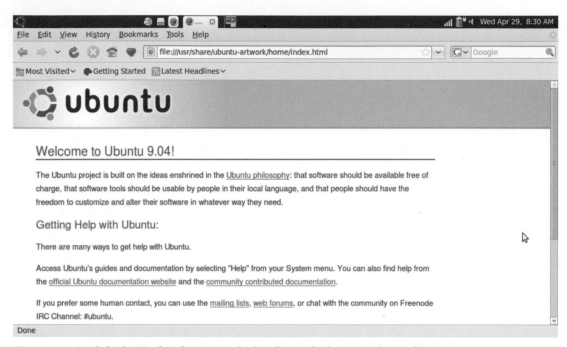

Figure 4-1. By default, Firefox shows you the local stored Ubuntu welcome file.

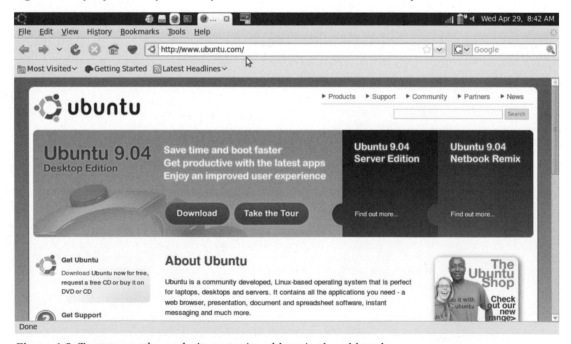

Figure 4-2. To go to another web site, enter its address in the address bar.

Optimizing the Firefox Display for Use on Your Netbook

When you're working with any application on a netbook, available display space on your screen is limited. Firefox has a simple solution: the F11 button, which helps maximize the display size. When you press F11, Firefox goes full screen. You no longer see the menu bar and buttons—the entire screen shows the contents of the browser. It's easy to get your menu back: move the cursor to the upper part of the window, and the menu bar and buttons reappear. Want to return to the normal display? Press F11 again. Figure 4-3 shows what Firefox looks like in full-screen mode.

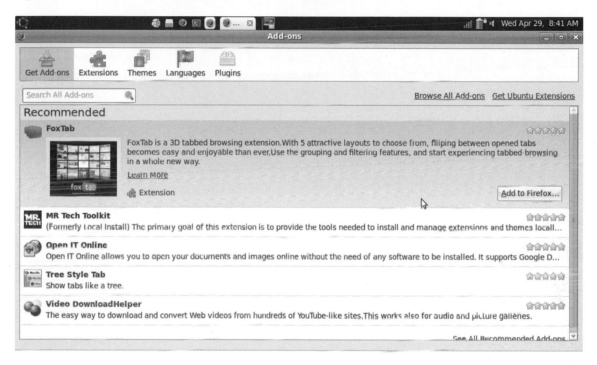

Figure 4-3. By pressing F11, you can work with Firefox in full-screen mode.

Working with Plugins, Add-ons, and Extensions

You'll often notice that a web server tries to deliver content that Firefox can't open by default. The most common reason for a web page not to work by default in Firefox is the use of Flash. To prevent this problem, you must install Flash. You can find more details about software installation in Chapter 8; for now, here's the procedure to get Flash by installing the Ubuntu Restricted Extras package:

1. Choose Accessories ➤ Add / Remove.

2. From the Show drop-down list, select All Available Applications. Type **restricted** in the Search box.

3. Ubuntu Restricted Extras appears first in the list. Select the check box next to it. This brings up a pop-up asking if you really want to install unsupported and restricted software. Click Enable. In the next pop-up, also click Enable.

79

4. The updated software index is downloaded. Click Apply Changes, and then click Apply.

The software is now installed, and you have Flash support.

If Flash wasn't the problem that was causing a web page not to work, you may need to install an extension. *Extensions* are useful additional programs that make the browser smarter and allow you to open content that isn't supported by default. Often, extensions for your browser are installed when you install a certain application. You can see which ones are installed by going to the Tools ➤ Add-ons menu option. Figure 4-3 shows you its available options.

■ **Note** The use of the words *add-ons*, *extensions*, and *plugins* may be confusing. *Add-on* is a catch-all term that includes extensions and plugins. There are lots of extensions and very few plugins, so you'll probably work most often with Firefox extensions.

The additional programs are offered via different tabs. The following categories are available:

- *Get Add-ons:* This tab provides an interface for searching and browsing all add-ons. These include the many available extensions that add new features, as well as alternative themes, additional language support, and plugins, including Java and Adobe Flash. Some examples of add-ons include the Video DownloadHelper, which captures video in a format that lets you save it to disk; and Adblock Plus, which helps you block advertisements in a smart way.

- *Extensions:* The Extensions tab is an interface for displaying and controlling the extensions you already have installed. You'll see some of the add-ons here that you installed using the Get Add-ons tab.

- *Themes:* These are templates that define what Firefox looks like. By default, you get the Default theme, but you can install other themes by using the Get Add-ons tab. The Themes tab shows a list of all themes that are currently installed.

- *Languages:* This tab provides support for multilingual environments.

- *Plugins: Plugins* are programs that allow you to handle content for programs that are non-native to Firefox. An example is the Adobe plugin that lets you read the content of PDF files directly from the browser. Plugins are often installed by running an installation procedure that also lets you install the stand-alone program.

As mentioned, an example of a useful extension is the Video DownloadHelper, which helps you download and convert videos from sites like YouTube. The Get Add-ons menu offers access to this add-on by default. The following procedure describes how you can install it:

1. From the Firefox main menu, choose Tools ➤ Add-ons.

2. Make sure the Get Add-ons option is selected, and click Video DownloadHelper. This shows you a short description of what this add-on is all about (see Figure 4-4).

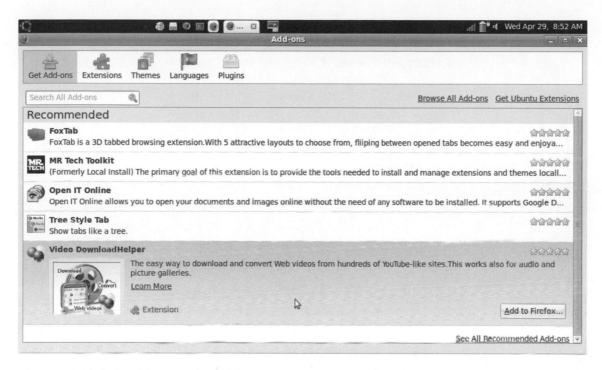

Figure 4-4. Click the Video DownloadHelper extension to see its description.

3. To add the extension to Firefox, click the Add to Firefox button in the lower-
    right corner of the window. The window shown in Figure 4-5 opens and asks if
    you really want to install this program. Click Install Now to install the
    extension.

Figure 4-5. Click Install Now to install the extension.

4.   The extension is added to the browser. To activate it, restart the browser.

Another way to add extensions and add-ons is to click the links in the upper-right corner of the Add-on window. For instance, the Get Ubuntu Extensions option shows you all extensions that are offered and maintained by Canonical or the Ubuntu community. Clicking one of these links starts the Add/Remove Applications program; see chapter 8 for more details on how to use this application. Another useful option is Browse All Add-ons, which opens a new tab in your browser and takes you to the Firefox Add-ons web site (see Figure 4-6). From this site, you can install any add-on you want. The following procedure describes you how:

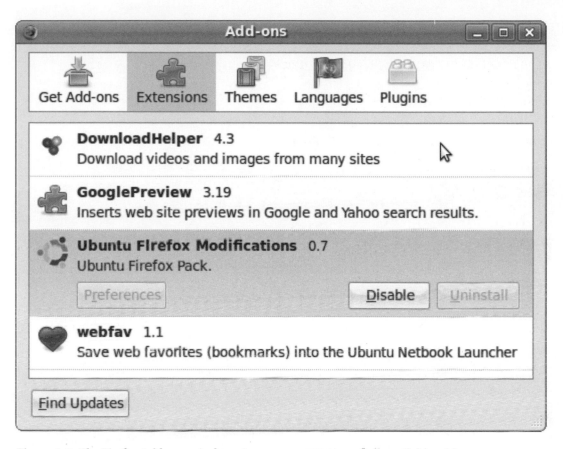

Figure 4-6. The Firefox Add-ons window gives you an overview of all available add-ons.

1. From the Firefox Add-ons menu option, select Browse All Add-ons. Doing so takes you to the Firefox Add-ons site.

2. Search, for example, for the GooglePreview option, and click Add to Firefox. The Software Installation window opens. Click Install Now to start the installation of the add-on.

3. When the process is complete, you're prompted to restart Firefox (see Figure 4-7).

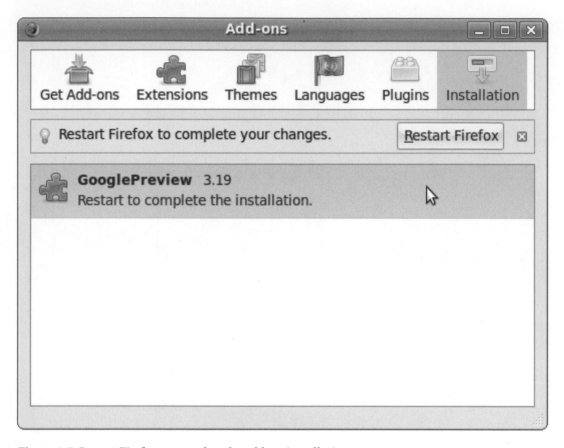

Figure 4-7. Restart Firefox to complete the add-on installation.

Setting Your Privacy Preferences

Managing privacy is a delicate affair, because increasing the privacy level too much may make it hard to do your work in a normal way. The optimal privacy settings offer you a balance between usability and protection. You can configure your privacy settings from the Edit ▶ Preferences menu option (see Figure 4-8).

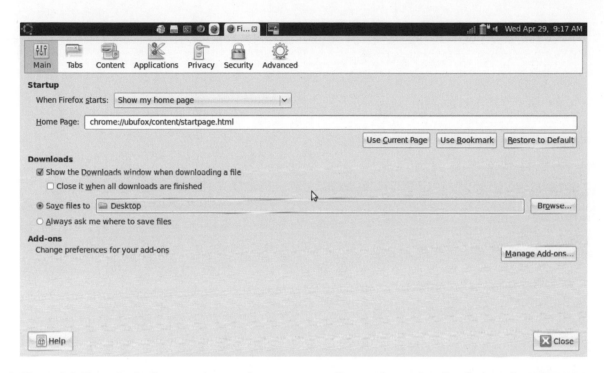

Figure 4-8. From the Preferences menu option, you can configure privacy related settings and much more.

The settings on the Privacy tab help you define what other people see when they access your computer. The options are divided into three categories (see Figure 4-9). First are the history-related options. By default, Firefox remembers the URLs you've recently visited. That means it's fairly easy for others to find out where you've been on the Internet and what you've downloaded. In some ways, keeping your history is convenient, because it allows features like auto-completion to do their work. On the other hand, it may be annoying, because it lets others see what you've done. You pay for convenience with your privacy—the choice is yours.

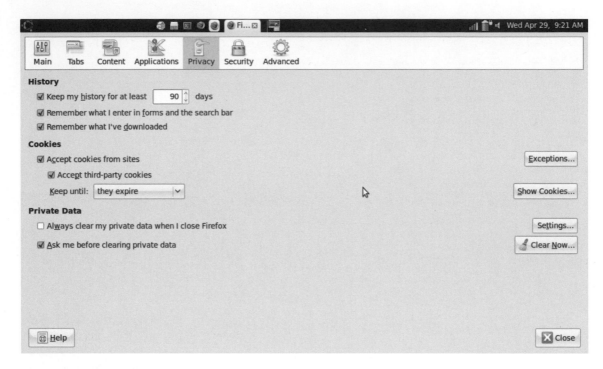

Figure 4-9. *The privacy settings are divided into three categories.*

Cookies are also useful and potentially intrusive at the same time. Cookies are small pieces of text that are stored on your computer to hold settings that you've recently used while visiting specific web sites. The next time you visit the same web site, the associated cookie may, for example, remember your password. Working with cookies can be dangerous because they may store personal data. For that reason, you may choose not to keep cookies on your computer. You can switch them off if you want to: choose Edit ➤ Preferences, and, on the Privacy tab, deselect the options "Accept cookies from sites" and "Accept third-party cookies." But note that if you switch cookies off, half the web will cease to work for you.

The third part of the privacy-related settings in Firefox helps you specify what you want to do with your private data, including cookies and other items such as your browsing history. As the default setting, Firefox always keeps your private data, because it may be useful when accessing the same site again or when restarting Firefox. If you don't like that setting, perhaps because you share your computer with others, you can select the option "Always clear my private data when I close Firefox." This makes sure nothing is ever kept on your computer's hard drive. From the Privacy menu, you can also click Clear Now to remove all privacy-related data instantly.

Firefox also provides a nice half-way solution. Choose Edit ➤ Preferences ➤ Privacy. There, you find the Keep Until drop-down list. From that list, select "Ask me every time." You'll get a warning the first time a site offers you cookies, and you'll have the option to accept them permanently from that site or for that session, or deny for the session or always.

■ **Tip** You don't have to use the Privacy menu to clear your private data. If you want to clear this data at any time while surfing the Web, the keyboard shortcut to use is Ctrl-Shift-Delete.

Setting Firefox Security Options

Security is closely related to privacy. In the Firefox security settings, you can define what happens when you're at a possibly dangerous web site. The default options on the Security tab, which you access from Edit ➤ Preferences, protect you as well as they can. Figure 4-10 shows the default settings.

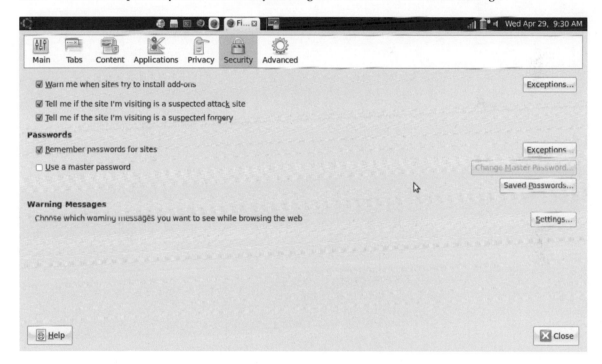

Figure 4-10. By default, Firefox offers good security settings.

I advise you not to change the security settings. They don't stop any threat completely, but they give you a warning if something happens that is potentially suspicious and ask if want to carry on.

A useful option on the Security tab that you may want to consider changing is "Use a master password." When you enable this option, you don't have to remember passwords for each individual web site—you can access all web sites that are protected with a password by entering one master password. Firefox stores the individual passwords for you (which of course may also be a risk).

Working with the Search Bar

Another useful feature that Firefox offers is the search bar in the upper-right corner of the program window. By using this search bar, you can search for items on the Internet. By default, the Google search engine is used for that purpose; but you can use the drop-down list next to the Google icon to select other web sites and search engines as well. These include pure search engines, such as Yahoo, as well as popular web sites such as Wikipedia and Amazon.com. Figure 4-11 shows the sites that appear by default in the drop-down list.

Figure 4-11. The search bar allows you to search in an easy way on different popular web sites.

You can also customize the default list of search engines that Ubuntu offers. To do this, select the Manage Search Engines option. This brings up the window shown in Figure 4-12. From this window, you can modify the search order that is used by clicking either Move Up or Move Down after selecting a search engine. Alternatively, you can use the "Get more search engines" option to add additional engines. The latter option takes you to the Firefox web site, where you can add new search engines by selecting an appropriate add-on.

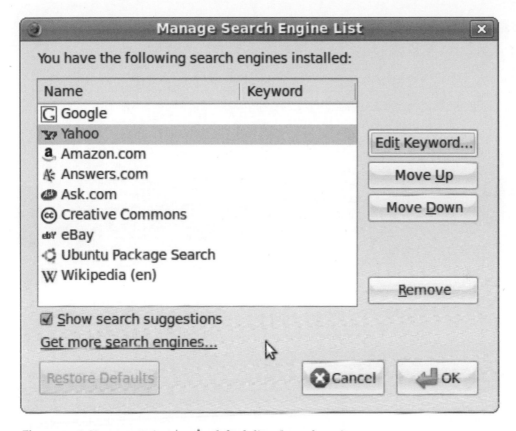

Figure 4-12. You can customize the default list of search engines.

Working with Bookmarks

One of the features that makes working with Firefox really convenient is bookmarks. A *bookmark* gets your browser to note the location of a page you like. After you've marked a page with a bookmark, you can use the bookmark as a link to easily get back to that page. To navigate back to the bookmarked page, select the bookmark from the Bookmarks menu.

Setting a bookmark is easy. Make sure you're on the page for which you want to create the bookmark, and press Ctrl-D to mark the page. This brings up the Edit This Bookmark window, in which you can enter a name, a folder, and some tags for the bookmarked page (see Figure 4-13).

Figure 4-13. *In the Edit This Bookmark window, you can enter properties for the bookmarked page to help you find the bookmark easily and remember what it is.*

Suppose you have another computer that runs Firefox and that already has lots of bookmarks in place. Wouldn't it be nice if you could synchronize the bookmarks on the other computer with this computer in an easy and convenient way? You can, with the help of the Xmarks add-on. To add it, select Tools ➤ Add-ons, and click Get Add-ons. In the search field, type **xmarks**; then, click Xmarks in the search results window. Now, click Add to Firefox (see Figure 4-14) and follow the prompts to add Xmarks to your browser.

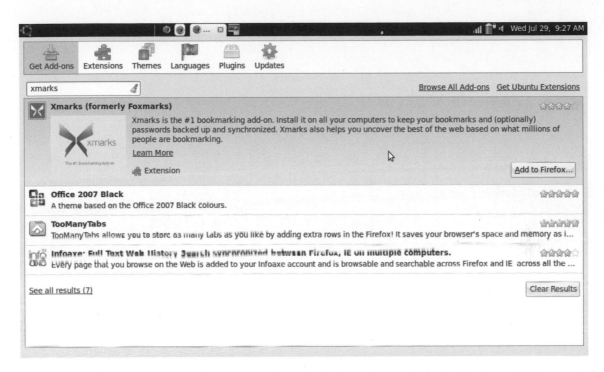

Figure 4-14. The Xmarks add-on helps you synchronize bookmarks and other personal settings between different computers.

After installing the Xmarks add-on, you need to restart Firefox. After you do, you'll see a "Click here to finish installing Xmarks" window. Clicking the button brings up a wizard that helps you set up Xmarks. In this wizard, click Next to start the configuration.

One of the most important parts of the Xmarks configuration is creating an Xmarks account. That account saves your settings on the Web, so that the Firefox browser on each of your computers can connect to your settings easily. Enter your account details, and click Next to continue (see Figure 4-15).

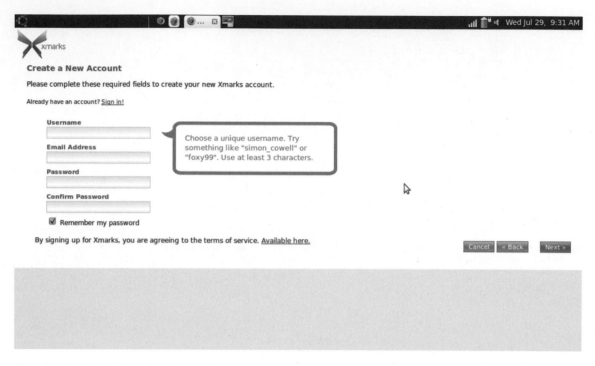

Figure 4-15. To use Xmarks, you need to create an Xmarks account on the Internet.

After creating the Xmarks account, you can specify what the add-on should do. Xmarks can synchronize not only bookmarks but passwords as well. If you want to synchronize passwords, you also need to enable secure password sync. Figure 4-16 shows the interface from which to do that. To protect your passwords, you need to enter a PIN code. This code is used to ensure the confidentiality of your passwords and makes sure you're the only one who can read the passwords. Make this a good password—it's all there is between the Internet and a whole collection of your passwords.

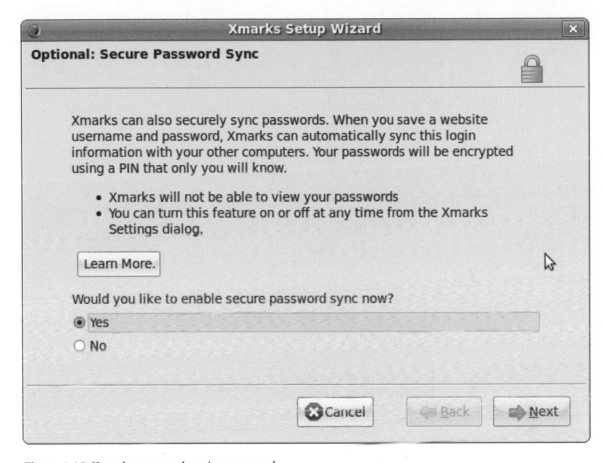

Figure 4-16. Xmarks can synchronize passwords.

When you've completed the Xmarks configuration, repeat these steps on all your other computers that use Firefox. From now on, you'll be able to access the same bookmarks on all computers you're using.

You now know enough about Firefox to get started using it on your netbook. You can configure and change lots more items in Firefox, but this should be plenty to get you going. In the next section, you'll learn how to handle e-mail on your netbook.

Working with Mail and Calendar

Sure, you can create a Google Mail account and do everything you must do online. Sometimes, however, it's also convenient if you have what you need with you, so you can look up important mail messages when you're offline. To do that, web mail isn't the most convenient solution. Even if Gmail is now capable of saving your messages for offline access, you may want to do more. The default solution is Evolution.

Evolution is much more than just a mail program. It's a fully featured personal information management program that allows you to handle mail, your calendar, and task lists. Given its functionality, it can easily compete with similar programs, such as Microsoft Outlook.

To handle mail with Evolution, you first need a mail account. Let's assume it's a mail account offered by your Internet provider. Typically, the Internet provider offers you two different ways to access your mail: the POP3 protocol, which you use to download mail to your computer; and IMAP, which you use to work with your mail while connected. Currently, POP3 offers online features via a webmail interface, and IMAP lets you synchronize mail from your provider to your local computer so you can access it if you're not online. But in the end, it all depends on the options your provider offers.

Creating a Mail Account in Evolution

Because the netbook may not be your primary computer, it's probably not a good idea to work with a solution that downloads all mail to your computer. I personally like POP a lot, because it's simple and it lets you read your mail when you aren't connected. A good solution is to set up a POP account and tell it not to delete mail messages from your server. This allows you to connect to the same POP account later, on your main computer, and download the messages there. In the following example, you'll learn how to create a POP mail account for an example user named Linda:

1. Choose Internet ➤ Evolution Mail. This starts the Evolution Mail program shown in Figure 4-17. If this is the first time you start Evolution, it will open a Setup Assistant. Click Forward.

■ **Note** if your netbook has a very small screen, the Evolution Setup Assistant is too big to fit on the screen. If that happens on your computer, remember that you can use the Alt-F7 key sequence and move the window by using the arrow keys to put it in focus.

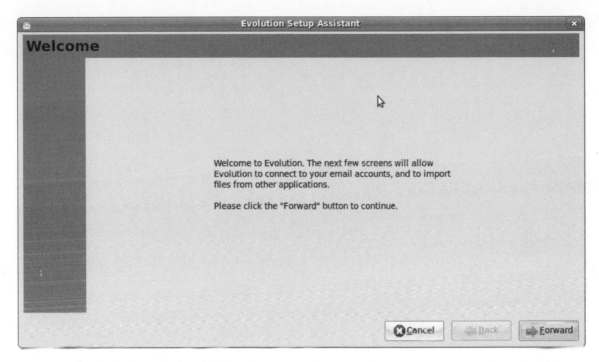

Figure 4-17. The first time you start Evolution, a Setup Assistant opens.

2. If you want to import mail from a backup file that you've created using Evolution at another computer, select the "Restore Evolution from the backup file" option (see Figure 4-18), and browse to the location where you stored this backup file. Next, click Apply.

■ **Tip** If you want to import data from another mail or calendar program thta is saved in a standard format such as mbox for mail or vcal / ical for calendars, you can use File ➤ Import after you have Evolution completely operational.

Figure 4-18. You can import mail from Evolution on another computer if you've stored that mail in a backup file.

3. If you haven't imported a backup file, enter your personal information in the next step of the procedure. The minimum you should enter are a full name and an e-mail address. Optionally, you can also enter a reply address (where answers to this mail will be automatically sent) and the name of the organization you work for (see Figure 4-19). Click Forward.

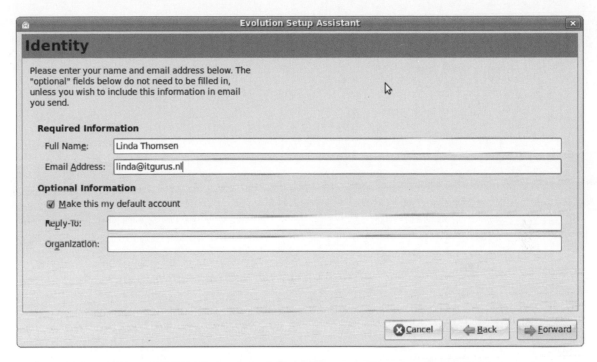

Figure 4-19. As a minimal requirement, you need to enter your full name and e-mail address.

4. Specify which type of server you're using. As you can see from the drop-down list in Figure 4-20, different server types are supported; you can, for instance, connect to a Novell GroupWise mail server in a corporate environment. The final choice is determined by the type of mail server you're using. In most cases, this will be either POP or IMAP. Because the user in this demo scenario uses POP (which is the case for most Internet mail), select POP from the drop-down list. Click Forward.

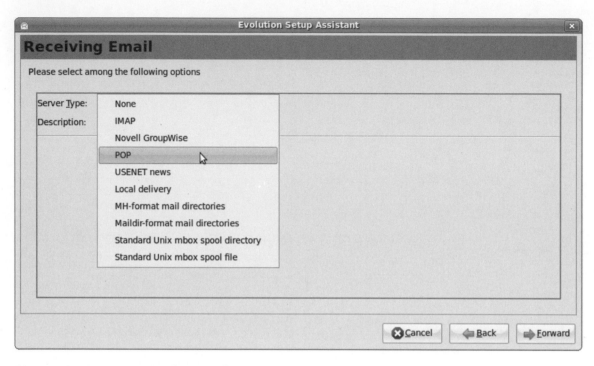

Figure 4-20. For Internet mail, POP is the most common mail server type.

5. You're prompted to enter the information needed to connect to the type of mail server you selected in step 4. Normally, that will be the domain name of the server you need to connect to, the type of security used (encryption or no encryption), and the type of password (see Figure 4-21). Your Internet provider can give you all the information you need. In most cases, you can use "No encryption" as the default security setting (which means your mail isn't encrypted and can be sniffed for passwords and other sensitive information while it's being sent). Mail servers that required SSL or TLS encryption by default are rare. To find out what kind of password your mail server requires, click the Check for Supported Types button. Doing so contacts your mail server directly to find out what kind of password you need to use.

    Also very convenient is the "Remember password" option. Use this option to make sure you don't have to enter your password again and again, every time you connect to your mail server. When you're finished with this step, click Forward.

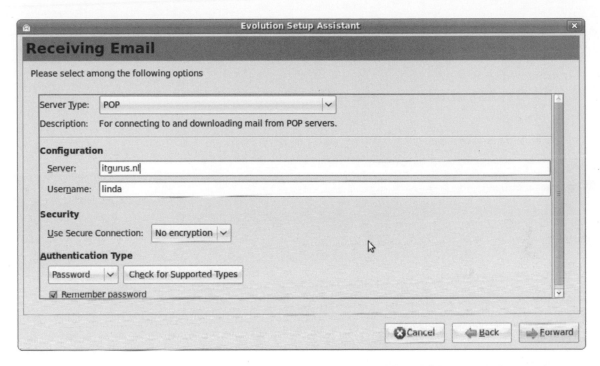

Figure 4-21. You need at least the name of the server and the name of the user account on that mail server.

6. You need to specify your mail-receiving options (see Figure 4-22). First, you can indicate whether you want Evolution to check for new mail automatically from time to time. If you do, select the "Check for new messages every *N* minutes" option, and specify how often it should check.

You may also want to use the "Leave messages on server" option. This option is useful if the netbook computer isn't your primary computer. It lets you download mail messages to your primary computer later. If the netbook is your primary computer, selecting this option makes no sense. Click Forward.

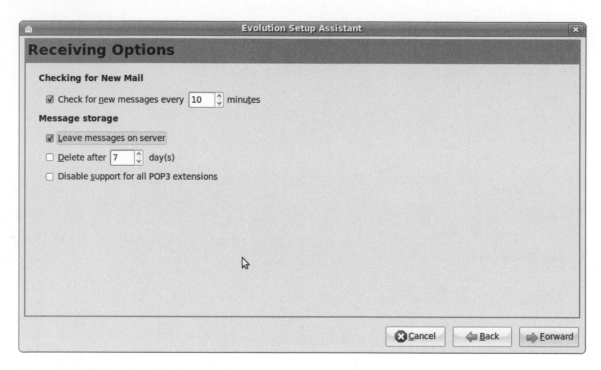

Figure 4-22. If the netbook isn't your primary computer, it may be useful to leave the mail messages on the server.

7. You also need to specify how you want to send messages (see Figure 4-23). In the Server Type drop-down list, you have two options: SMTP and Sendmail. In almost all cases, you'll need SMTP. Select it, and then tell the program the name of your mail server. Note that often, this isn't the same as the name of the server you're using to receive mail.

To allow you to send e-mail, many mail servers require authentication. This normally means you must enter the same username and password required to receive e-mail as well. If you're not sure how to authenticate, click the Check for Supported Types button to find out what authentication type your server requires. Then, click Forward to proceed to the next step of the configuration.

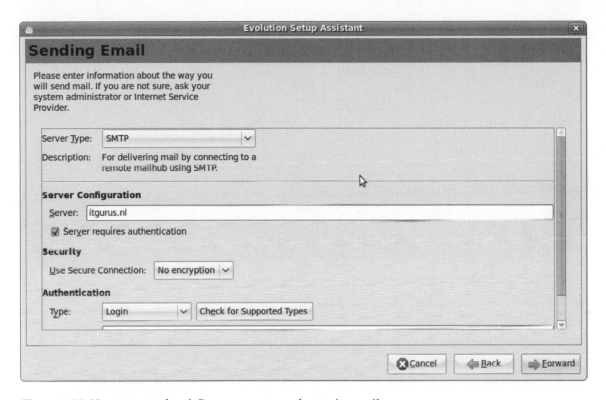

Figure 4-23. Now, you need to define a server to send outgoing mail.

8. Enter a name for the account. By default, the name of the mail address you're using is used here. If you want to change it, do so, and then click Forward to continue. There isn't much need to change the name, because it's used only to distinguish between different mail servers you may be using. Click Forward.

9. Click the world map to tell Evolution which time zone you're in. Selecting the proper time zone makes sure the dates on your incoming and outgoing mail messages are set as they should be. Click Forward.

10. You see the last page of the Setup Assistant. Click Finish to complete the configuration. Doing so automatically launches the Evolution main window, where you're prompted to enter a password for the mail account you just created (see Figure 4-24).

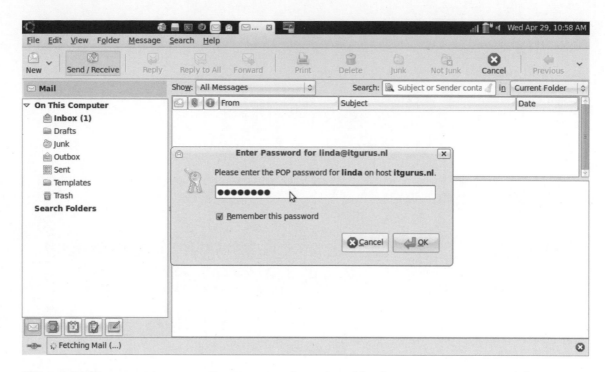

Figure 4-24. *To connect to your mail server, enter the password for the user account you created.*

Sending and Receiving Mail

Now that you've set up your mail account, you can begin sending and receiving e-mail. At least one message should be waiting for you: a welcome message that is created by default by the Evolution mail program. You may also have received other messages. You can see the contents of the message by clicking the message title in the inbox (see Figure 4-25). If the display is too small to read the message, double-click the message in the inbox to open it fullscreen (see Figure 4-26).

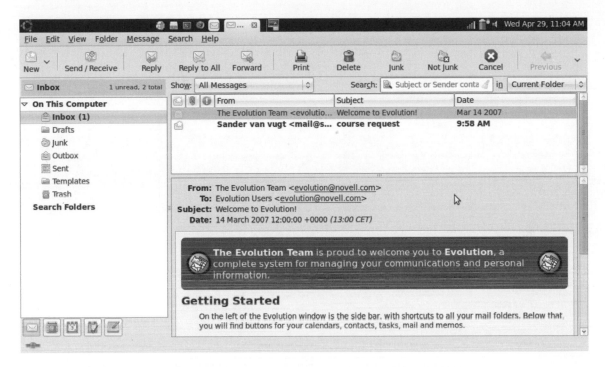

Figure 4-25. *Click the message title in the inbox to read the contents of the message.*

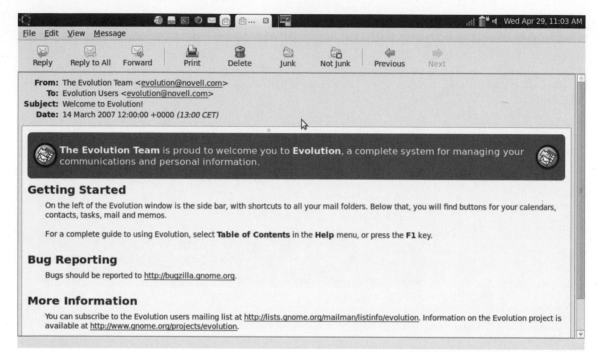

Figure 4-26. Double-clicking the message listing in the inbox opens the contents fullscreen.

To reply to an existing message, make sure it's selected, and then click the Reply button. This opens a window containing the text of the old message; from here, you can reply to the message you've received.

To create a new mail message, click the New button. Doing so opens the mail-composition window, where you can compose the new message. As you use Evolution, your address book will fill automatically with the e-mail addresses of all the people to whom you've sent e-mail messages. At this point, however, it's probably empty, so you must type the complete address (make sure it looks like this: someone@example.com). Next, type a subject and a message, and click the Send button to send the message (see Figure 4-27).

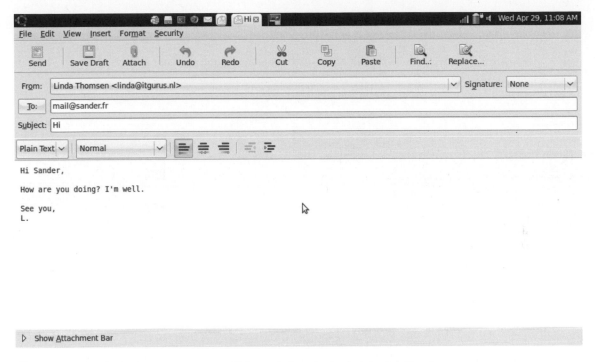

Figure 4-27. Evolution's message-composition window has a simple, familiar layout.

Depending on whether you asked Evolution to remember your password, you may now have to enter a password. After you do that, the message is sent to the intended recipient.

Managing Your Schedule with Evolution

In addition to letting you send and receive mail, Evolution offers some other useful functionality. One of these features is the calendar, which allows you to manage your meetings and appointments. The Calendars view gives you an overview of all your appointments for today, including a list of tasks you must perform (which you can also manage with Evolution) and memos you've written.

To access your calendar, open the Calendars view by clicking the Calendars button in the lower-left part of the Evolution main window (see Figure 4-28).

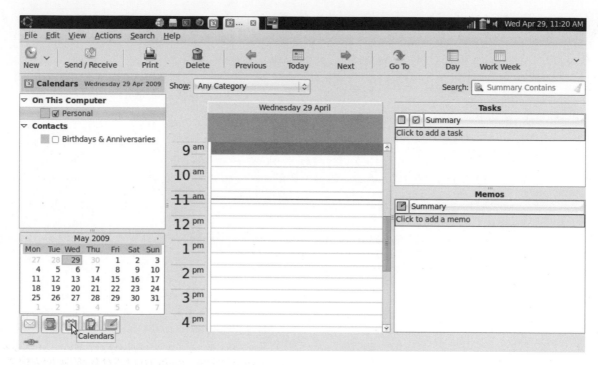

Figure 4-28. Click the Calendars button to access your current appointments.

In the Calendars view, you can add new appointments, new tasks, and new memos. The easiest way to add any of these is to use the options in the New menu. You can add three types of items in your calendar: appointments, meetings, and all-day appointments. The difference between an appointment and a meeting is that you can invite other people to a meeting. After you create a meeting, an invitation is sent to the people you've invited.

Creating a meeting isn't hard: choose New ➤ New Meeting to open the window shown in Figure 4-29. Enter the people you want to invite for this meeting, and provide a summary of what the meeting is about, a location, and a time. Click Save to save the meeting. You're prompted to say whether you want to send invitations. If you do so, a message goes out immediately to all meeting participants; they can reply to say whether they will be present.

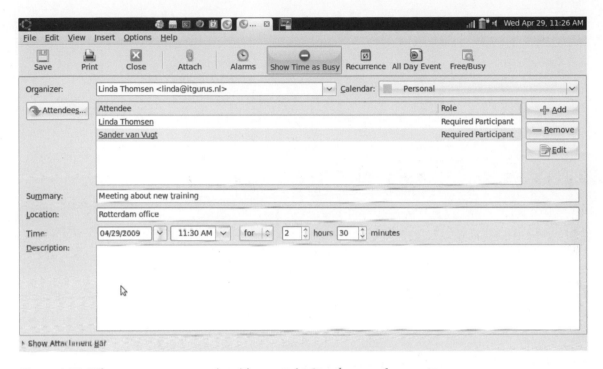

Figure 4-29. When you create a meeting, it's easy to invite other people.

Another useful item that the Evolution calendar offers is the option to add new calendars. For instance, you can connect to your Google calendar on the Internet. The following procedure describes how to do that:

1. From the Calendars view (see Figure 4-28), select New ➤ Calendar. Doing so opens the New Calendar window (see Figure 4-30).

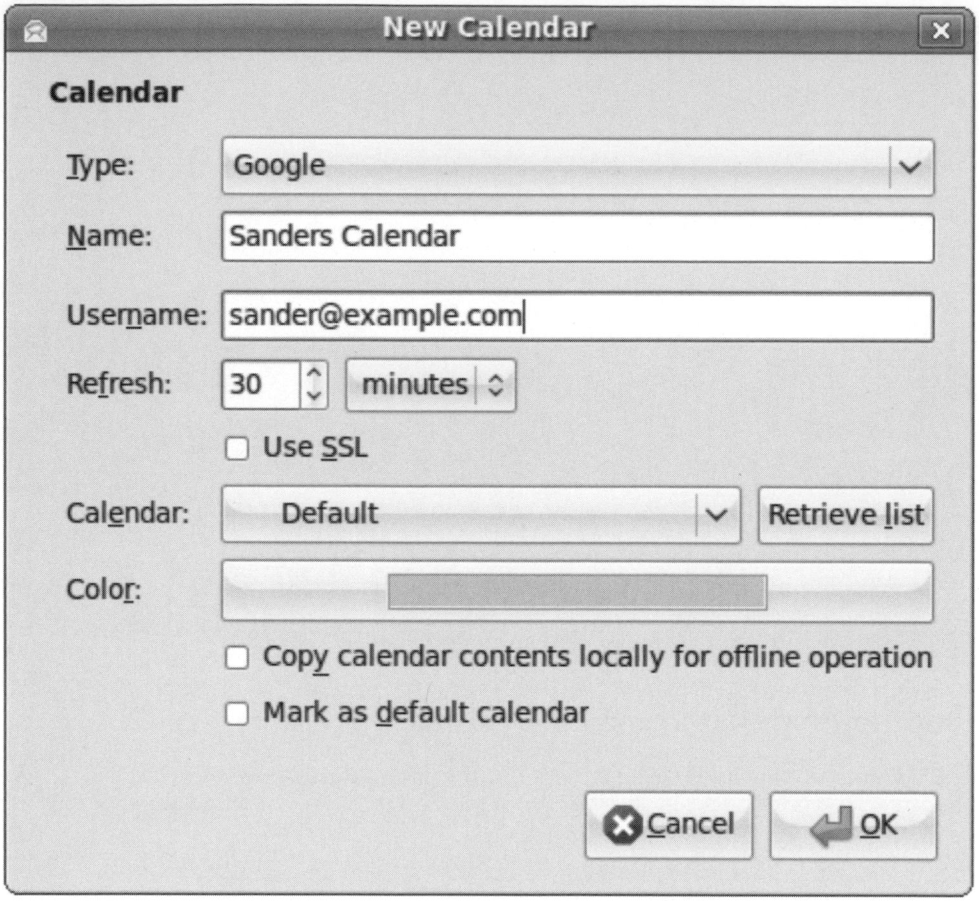

Figure 4-30. You can also import your Google calendar in Evolution.

2. From the Type drop-down list, select Google, and enter a name and a username for this calendar. The username is the Google account name associated with the Google calendar on the Internet. It's also useful to select the option "Copy calendar contents locally for offline operation," which ensures that you can also see your appointments from the external calendar if you're offline.

3. When prompted for a password, enter the password associated with your Google account. After you do so, your Google calendar is added to Evolution automatically.

■ **Tip** You can connect to your own calendar on the Internet, but the external calendar option lets you connect to others' calendars as well. That's useful if you need to work closely with someone.

A final cool item to add to Evolution is the current weather. Many people who work with computers are too busy to go outside (or look out the window) to see the current weather, so you can have Evolution tell you what the current weather is. This works for your location, and you can also add any other location on the planet. You do this by selecting New ➤ Calendar option in the Calendars view. From the Type list, select Weather (see Figure 4-31).

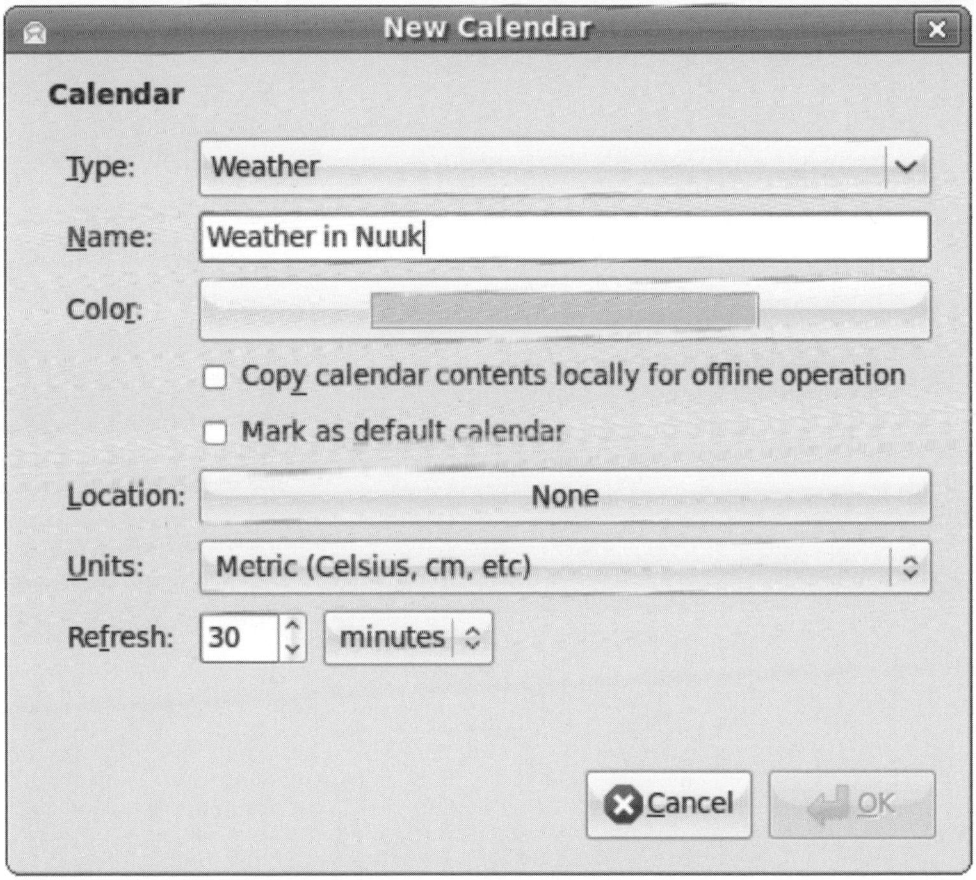

Figure 4-31. You can also add the current weather to Evolution.

109

Enter a name for your weather message, a color, and a location, and configure the units you want to use. The Units option lets you choose between Metric units (temperature in Celsius) and Imperial units (temperature in Fahrenheit). Click OK to apply these settings. You'll now see the current weather in Evolution's Today view.

Managing Tasks in Evolution

To enhance your productivity in the office, Evolution offers a task manager that integrates well in the Calendars view. If you prefer, you can open a dedicated Tasks view by clicking the Tasks button in the lower-left part of the Evolution window (see Figure 4-32).

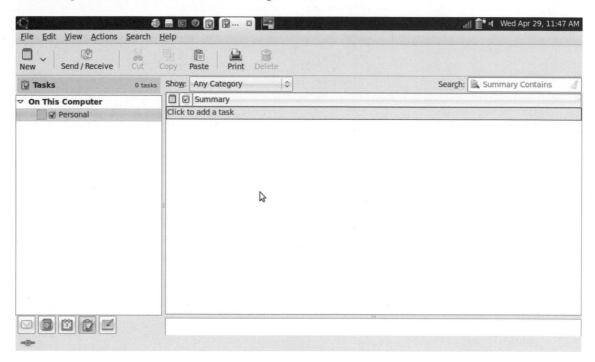

Figure 4-32. With Evolution, you can easily manage tasks.

By default, the Tasks display gives an overview of all current tasks. To add a new task, click the New task line in the Tasks view (which opens a Create Task summary screen); or, for a more complete overview, select New ➤ Task. Next, enter a short description of the task in the Summary field, and specify the task's start date and end date and an optional description. For instance, you can copy the contents of e-mail messages you've exchanged about this task into the Description field, to make it clear what the task is about. Click Save to add the task to the task list. You now have an easily accessible overview of all the tasks that you need to complete, any time you open the Tasks view or the Calendars view in Evolution.

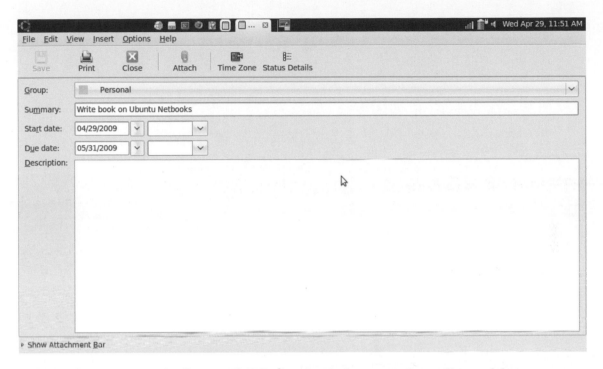

Figure 4-33. To create a task, all you need are a short description, a start date, and an end date.

Making Internet Phone Calls with Skype

If you have a Skype account, you can call other Skype users for free, using your Internet connection. The only requirement is that the person you're calling has Skype installed on their computer. If they don't, you can call their landline or mobile phone, but the call isn't free. However, Skype calling fees are very low—even if you must pay, a call costs no more than a few cents per minute. Hence, Skype is a valuable addition to your netbook computer.

By default, Skype isn't installed on Ubuntu Netbook Remix. In this section, you'll learn how to install Skype and how to use it to make an Internet phone call for free.

Installing Skype

You must download Skype from the Internet and install it by hand. The following procedure tells you how to do that:

1. Open Firefox, and go to http://packages.medibuntu.org (you can also get the Ubuntu Skype packages from the Skype web site).

2. Select the Ubuntu version you're using (if you need the latest version, choose the last one from the list); for Ubuntu 9.04, this is Jaunty.

3. From the list of packages, select the skype folder by clicking it.

4. In the Download Skype interface, choose the i386 version of the software, and click Save File to save the file to the desktop of your computer.

5. Repeat this procedure for the skype-common package.

6. Use the file browser to browse to your Desktop folder, which displays the names of all the files on your computer desktop. This includes the skype package as well as the skype-common package.

7. Right-click the skype-common package, and select Open with GDebi Package Installer.

8. In the Package Installer interface, click Install Package (see Figure 4-34). Enter your password to obtain administrator permissions to proceed.

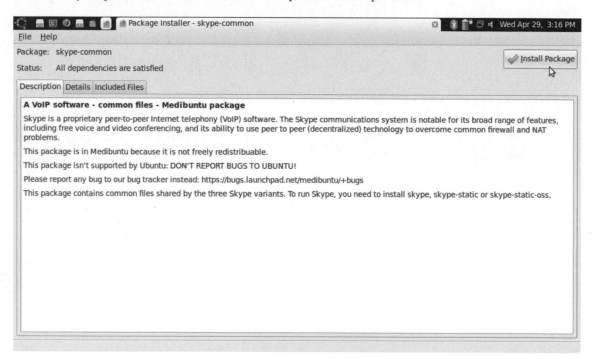

Figure 4-34. Click Install Package to install the skype-common package.

9. To use Skype, open the Internet menu, and click the newly added Skype icon (see Figure 4-35).

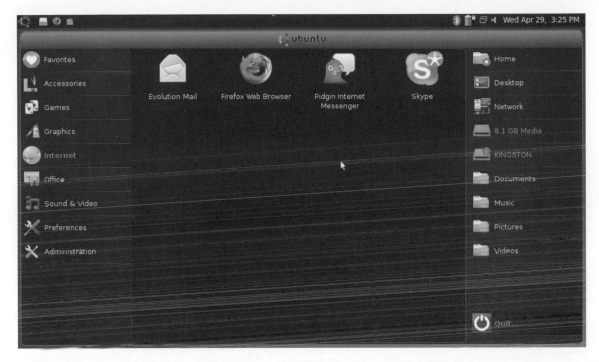

Figure 4-35. After succesful installation, a Skype icon is added to the Internet menu automatically.

Configuring Skype

Now that you have Skype installed, you need to configure it. To do this, you must have a Skype account. If you already have a Skype account, enter the account details to initialize the connection. If you don't have a Skype account, you need to create one. The following procedure explains how:

1. From the Internet menu, click the Skype icon to start Skype. A user license agreement opens; click Accept to accept its conditions.

2. The Welcome to Skype window opens (see Figure 4-36). If you already have a Skype username and password, enter them here to connect. If you don't have a username yet (which I'll assume here), click the "Don't have a Skype Name yet" link.

Figure 4-36. If you already have a Skype username, enter it here.

3. The Create a new Skype Account window opens. Enter your personal details, including your full name, your e-mail address, the Skype name you want to use, and a password. Also check that you agree to all Skype conditions. Then, click "Sign up" to set up the account (see Figure 4-37).

Figure 4-37. Enter your personal details and a Skype name of your choice to sign up with Skype.

4. Skype checks whether the Skype name of your choice is available. If it's not, you see a message to that effect, and you can try another name. When you've found an unused Skype account name, a Congratulations window opens. Click Close. The Skype account is created and activated, and you can begin using it.

Making Your First Phone Call with Skype

Now that you've successfully configured Skype, you can make your first phone call with it. I recommend making the Skype Test Call first. This is a default call that is presented automatically and that lets you test whether all the settings work as expected. Before you do this, I also recommend that you connect a headset. The average quality of the speakers and microphone in netbook computers isn't good, and using a headset will result in a better quality phone call. If you have a headset, connect it now, and then click the green button to make the test call from Skype (see Figure 4-38).

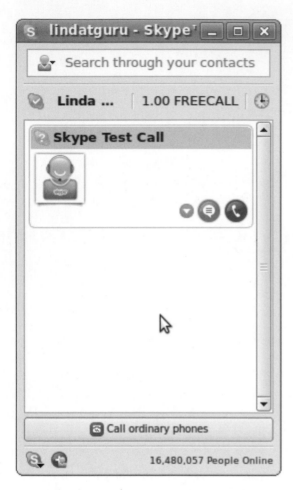

Figure 4-38. *Before making your first real phone call, make the Skype Test Call to verify that your hardware works.*

You may see a window that tells you about a problem with audio playback and/or the microphone. If this is the case, click the blue Skype icon in the lower-left corner of the Skype window, and select Options. Doing so opens the Options window shown in Figure 4-39. In this window, select the Sound Devices menu item.

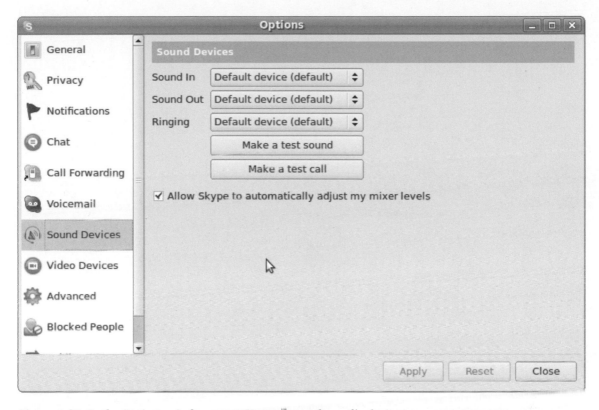

Figure 4-39. In the Options window, you can configure the audio devices on your computer.

In Figure 4-29, the default device is select for Sound In, Sound Out, and Ringing. If this default device doesn't work, you obviously must select something else. On my netbook computers, the HDA Intel (hw:intel,0) device works well, but this may be different in your case. After selecting alternative audio devices, click Make a test call to try the test call again. Repeat this procedure until you find a working device.

When you've configured your audio hardware, you may want to configure your video hardware as well. If the Skype Options window is still open, click the Video Devices option. A black screen with a Test button appears in the upper-right corner of the screen; click Test. Doing so activates your webcam, and you should see yourself (see Figure 4-40, with a picture of your friendly author). Next, you need to determine how you want to use the Skype video option. By default, people can only see you when you enable that option in a call (which normally is a good idea). But if you prefer, you can select the option "Start my video automatically when I am in a call." You have some options for receiving video as well. By default, you'll see video only for people you've allowed. If you wish, you can change the settings. When you're finished, click Apply to save your settings. Close the Skype Options window.

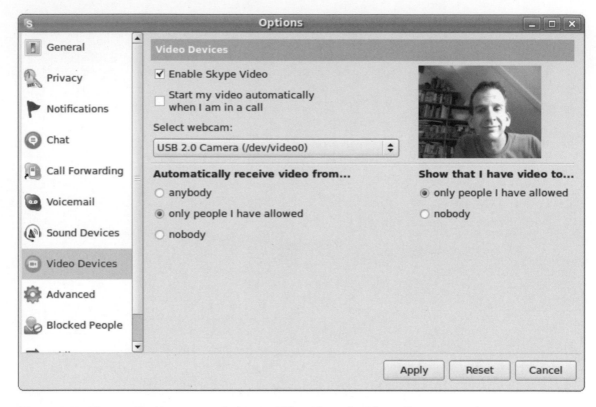

Figure 4-40. *After configuring your webcam, you'll be able to do video calls.*

Now that everything is working, you can make your first real phone call. To call people who are on Skype, click the Add a Skype Contact button at lower left in the Skype window. This opens a window in which you can search for the person you're looking for. Enter as many details as possible to increase the chances of finding this person (see Figure 4-41).

Figure 4-41. Enter as many details as possible about the person you're looking for.

When you find the person, select their name and click Add Contact (see Figure 4-42). Doing so sends them an invitation. Only after they accept your invitation will you see them online in your Skype contacts list. In the Say Hello To window, you can also add a personal message if you wish. Click OK to close this window and send the invitation.

Figure 4-42. Click the person you want to add to your contacts, and click Add Contact.

The new contact appears in your contact list (see Figure 4-43). To call them, click their name, and then click the green dial button. Alternatively, you can click the blue chat button to initiate a chat session. This is less intrusive, and it also allows you to communicate with the other person in real time.

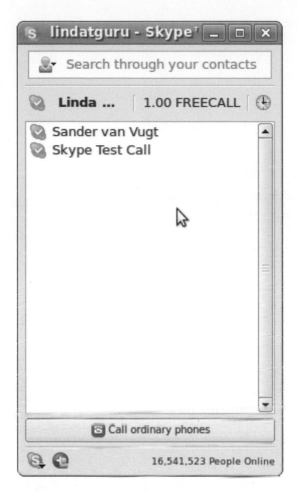

Figure 4-43. After your new contact has accepted your invitation, you can see if they're online in your contacts list.

Advanced Use of Skype

You now know how to use Skype to make phone calls to other people who also have Skype installed. Skype also offers some nice advanced methods of making calls. For instance, you can use Skype to call an ordinary phone, but not for free. You can make a short phone call to a landline; but if you want to continue using this functionality, you need to set up a SkypeOut account. After you make your first outgoing phone call, you see an indication of your current Skype balance in the Skype window. Click the balance; it shows that your SkypeOut account is currently inactive. To activate it, click the hyperlink (see Figure 4-44), and follow the additional configuration prompts on the Skype web site.

Figure 4-44. *Before you can use SkypeOut, you need to set up a SkypeOut account.*

Another useful feature of Skype is the option to set up a conference call. You can find this option in the Skype menu at lower left in the Skype window. Click it, and select Start Conference Call. You can now enter a topic for the conference call and invite people to join the call. To do so, click the names of the people you want to add, and then click Call to establish the call (see Figure 4-45). Using this feature, you can have meetings with more than one person online without paying anything.

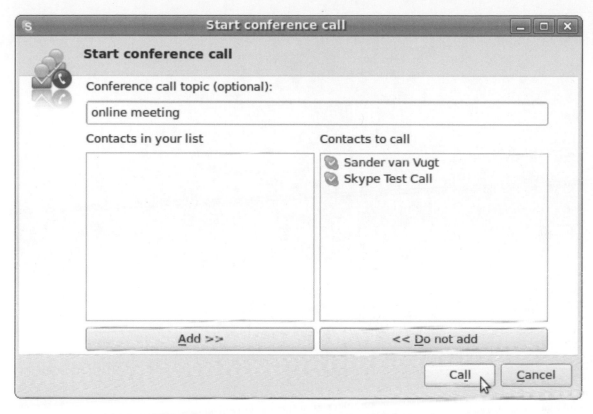

Figure 4-45. Skype allows you to have a conference call with others for free.

Managing Your Status

There's one more useful thing that you should know about Skype: you can use it to manage your current status. That way, your contacts can see whether you're available before they try to call you on Skype. To do this, right-click the green Skype icon on your netbook's toolbar, and select Change Status from the drop-down menu (see Figure 4-46).

Figure 4-46. If you don't want to be disturbed, you can let others know by changing your current status.

As you can see, several Skype status indicators are available. Here's a short list with a description for each one:

- *Online:* You're available, and others can Skype you.

- *Skype Me:* The entire world can see that you're available to receive Skype calls. Using this option will encourage total strangers to call you. You must have time for this, but if you do, it can lead to interesting new contacts. A friend of mine found his new bride this way!

- *Away:* You're not currently available. Your status changes to Away automatically if you haven't worked on your computer for a while.

- *Not Available:* Your computer is on, but you're currently not available. Use this, for example, if your computer is downloading files in the middle of the night while you're sleeping.

- *Do Not Disturb:* This option speaks for itself. Use it if you're in a meeting.

- *Invisible:* Other people can't see you, but you can see them. Use this option if you don't want to be disturbed and also don't want others to see that you're online.

- *Offline:* This option disconnects your Skype instance from the Skype network, which makes sure no one can disturb you.

Instant Messaging with Pidgin

If you've installed Skype, you already have a decent instant messaging solution installed on your computer. The essence of instant messaging is that people sign in to an instant messaging (IM) network. From there, they can see other people who have signed in to the same IM network, if those people let others see that they're online.

The problem with IM today is that there are so many IM networks. Pidgin tries to offer a solution to that issue. It's an integrated IM client that lets you connect to different IM networks simultaneously. When you start using Pidgin, the days are over when you need several IM clients on your computer, all open at the same time. The following procedure shows how to configure it:

1. From the Internet menu, click Pidgin. Doing so starts Pidgin and opens the Accounts window, where you can enter all of your IM accounts (see Figure 4-47).

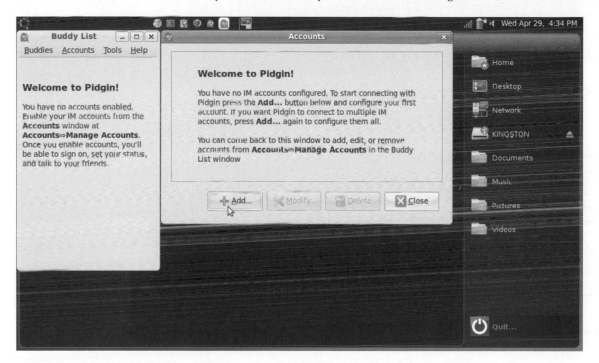

Figure 4-47. Click Add to begin configuring your IM accounts.

2. The Add Account window lets you select the protocol for which you want to configure an account. As you can see in Figure 4-48, many protocols are supported; a couple of your IM network solutions are probably listed by default.

125

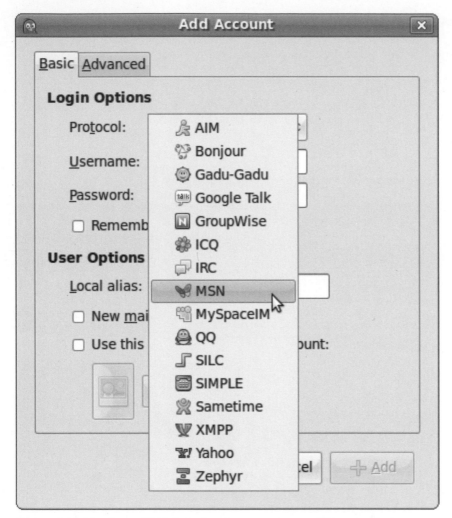

Figure 4-48. The force of Pidgin is that it supports many IM protocols.

3. After you enter all IM accounts you want to use, you're ready to use IM with Pidgin. You'll see all your buddies listed in the Pidgin Buddy List. Happy chatting!

Summary

In this chapter, you've learned how to use some important Internet applications on your netbook. You now know how to configure Firefox to work with plugins and how to specify security and privacy settings. You've also learned how to set up an e-mail account in Evolution. Following that, you read how to use Skype to make free phone calls on the Internet and how you can configure the Pidgin IM client as an integrated instant messaging solution for many different networks. In the next chapter, you'll learn how to do your office work with your netbook.

CHAPTER 5

■■■

Creating Office Files

One of the things you'll soon appreciate on your netbook is the ability to do your work anywhere. This is especially true for 10-inch models, which have keyboards large enough for most hands to use without much trouble. An important aspect of most people's work is creating office documents. Ubuntu Netbook Remix comes with the office suite OpenOffice.org. In this chapter, you'll get an introduction to using this office suite. The following topics are covered:

- Exploring OpenOffice.org

- Ensuring compatibility with Microsoft Office

- Becoming familiar with specific OpenOffice.org features

Exploring OpenOffice.org

You've probably created documents with an office suite before—probably Microsoft Office. You'll soon notice that OpenOffice.org offers an interface that is similar to the Microsoft Office interface, and that you can accomplish almost every task with OpenOffice.org that you can accomplish with Microsoft Office. Hence, transitioning from Microsoft Office to OpenOffice.org isn't difficult.

In this chapter, I won't explain how to work with an office solution from scratch; instead, I'll focus on the particulars of OpenOffice.org and the items required to get going as soon as possible. You can find the OpenOffice.org applications in the launcher's Office application group, together with some other applications that aren't part of OpenOffice.org (see Figure 5-1).

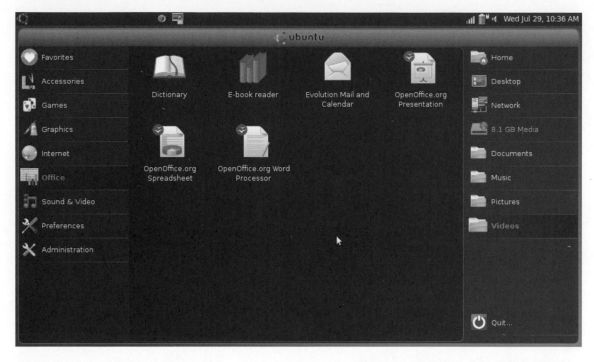

Figure 5-1. You can find the OpenOffice.org applications in the Office application group in the launcher.

Before you begin working with OpenOffice.org, you should become familiar with its nature. First, OpenOffice.org is an integrated office suite. That means its main components are linked to each other. This makes your work with OpenOffice.org as easy as it can possibly get. The following are the most important applications:

- Word processor (Writer)
- Spreadsheet (Calc)
- Presentation (Impress)

■ **Note** Every application in GNOME has a generic name that refers to its functionality and also a brand name. For instance, the file browser you read about in Chapter 2 is named Nautilus. Likewise, the OpenOffice.org applications have brand names. The GNOME convention, however, is not to talk about these brand names but to create icons that refer to an application's primary functionality. You'll notice this when working with OpenOffice.org applications as well. For instance, if you choose the Word Processor application, its brand name (Writer) appears in the menu bar and help menus. The same is true for the Spreadsheet (Calc) and Presentation (Impress) applications.

When you're working with OpenOffice.org Writer, you use the interface shown in Figure 5-2. Calc and Impress give you a similar interface. In this interface, all tasks are available as menu options, and some of the most important tasks are accessible through buttons on the button bar. Here are descriptions of the available menu options:

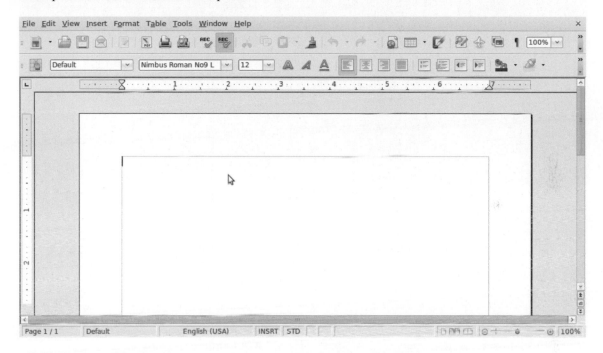

Figure 5-2. In any OpenOffice.org application, you'll find all the important options on the menus.

- *File:* This menu contains all options related to the file(s) you create with OpenOffice.org, such as saving a document to a file, open existing documents, and printing documents. From the File menu you can also access several wizards that make it easy for you to create certain document types (see Figure 5-3).

129

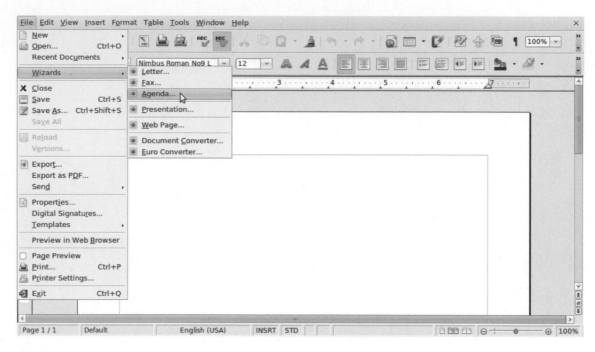

Figure 5-3. Using one of the available wizards, it's easy to create certain document types.

- *Edit:* This menu offers generic editing options that you can find in virtually all applications, such as Cut, Copy, and Paste. You'll also find options that apply to your specific document. For instance, you can add footnotes, find and replace text, or undo your last action if you aren't happy with it.

- *View:* These let you see different items in your document. For example, you can determine what you see on your computer desktop, and whether you see a ruler that indicates measures and distances in your current document. Using the options in this menu lets you maximize the screen-resolution efficiency of your work with OpenOffice.org in Ubuntu Netbook Remix.

■ **Tip** When you're working on a 9-inch netbook, you'll probably have the impression that you don't see enough on the computer's display. To maximize your visual working area, select View ➤ Toolbars, and switch off all toolbars (see Figure 5-4). Doing so gives you a decent amount of working space in OpenOffice.org. Alternatively, you can use the Ctrl-Shift-J key sequence, which puts OpenOffice.org into full-screen mode. To return to the standard view, press the Escape key.

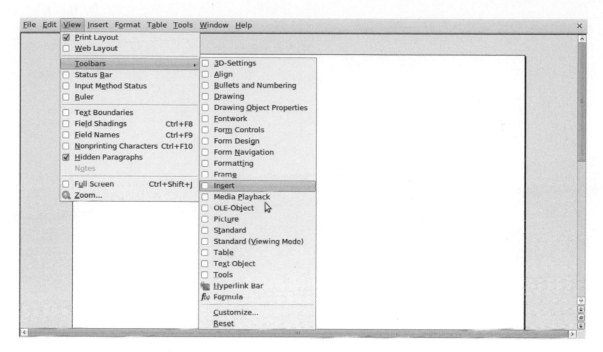

Figure 5-4. *By switching off all toolbars, you can maximize the visual working area on your computer's display.*

- *Insert:* This is probably the most important menu when you're laying out a document. From this menu, you can add items to your document such as pictures, the contents of files, index markers, headers, footers, and much more. The exact options depend on the application you're working with. Especially useful are the options available under Field; they let you add intelligent fields to your document, such as page numbers or the date when you last modified the document.

- *Format:* To create a document using the proper typesetting and paragraph layout, you can use the options on the Format menu. This menu offers different options depending on the application you're working with. For instance, the options in Writer under Format ➤ Character allow you to select a specific font type; and the items under Format ➤ Paragraph let you specify the exact layout of paragraphs. In Calc, the Format menu gives you all you need to specify the appropriate cell layout (see Figure 5-5).

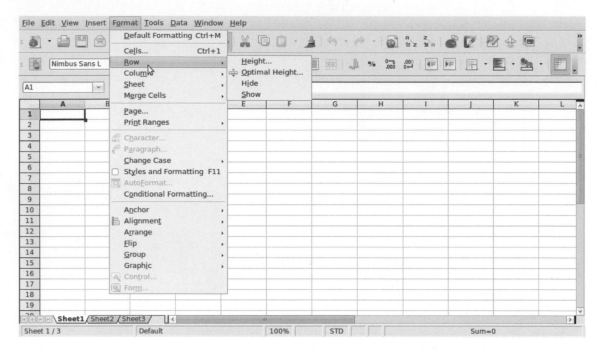

Figure 5-5. In Calc, the items on the Format menu let you specify exactly what cell layout to use.

- *Table:* The Table menu appears in the word processor but not in the spreadsheet application. It allows you to insert tables in your text document. You can also use the options on this menu to insert complex mathematical formulas.

- *Tools:* The items on the Tools menu give you access to useful additional programs. These include options like autocorrect and a spelling and grammar check, but also more advanced options like the Mail Merge Wizard, which helps you prepare e-mail messages to be sent to many recipients. Also in this menu, you'll find the Options item, which lets you set specific preferences for OpenOffice.org (see Figure 5-6).

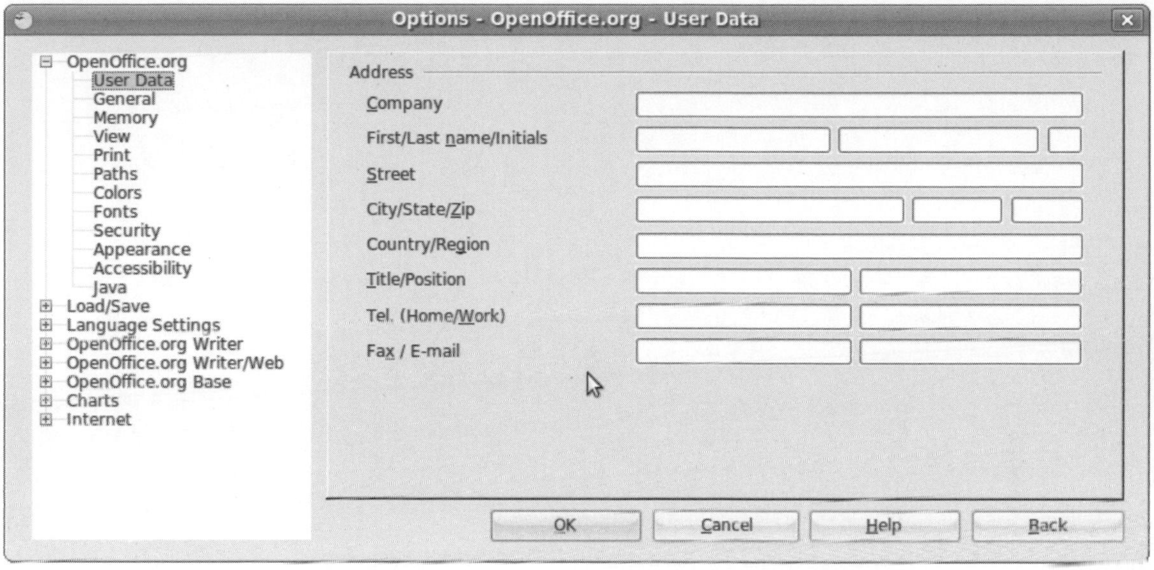

Figure 5-6. The Options item allows you to set specific preferences for working with OpenOffice.org.

- *Window:* The options in the Window menu help you work with the different components of OpenOffice.org. If you have different applications from the suite open at the same time, you can switch between them with the options on this menu. This also works if you have more than one document open. In addition, you can open a new program window or close the current window.

- *Help:* As its name suggests, this menu provides help on the different tasks you can perform with OpenOffice.org. If you've worked with electronic help in an application before, you won't have a hard time using these options.

One item on the Help menu deserves special attention: Translate This Application. This option shows the true open source nature of OpenOffice.org. You can use it if you're fluent in any language other than English and you want to help make OpenOffice.org available in your language. Selecting this option starts your browser and takes you to a web page where you find more information about helping to translate OpenOffice.org (see Figure 5-7).

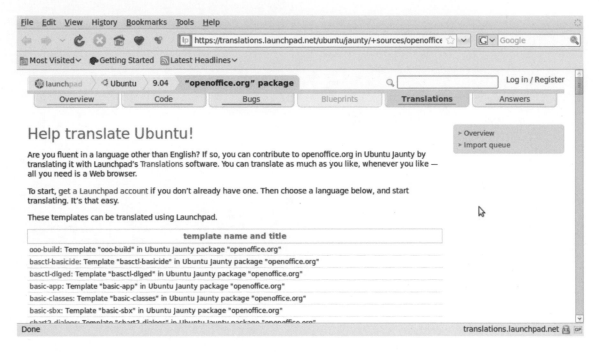

Figure 5-7. If you want to contribute to the open source spirit of OpenOffice.org, you can help translate it into languages other than English.

Ensuring Compatibility with Microsoft Office

While using OpenOffice.org, you'll sometimes have to work with people who instead use other office suites, such as Microsoft Office. You don't have to do much to share work with Microsoft Office users. To read documents created with Microsoft Office, you can open them in OpenOffice.org, regardless of the application you're using. Even modern XML-based Microsoft Office documents (such as the .docx documents created in Word 2007) open without problems in OpenOffice.org.

You need to be careful, however, when saving documents in OpenOffice.org, provided you want Microsoft Office users to be able to read them. The default OpenOffice.org format isn't supported in Microsoft Office, so you must make sure to save the documents to a format that Microsoft Office can read. This isn't hard to accomplish, and the procedure is basically the same for all OpenOffice.org applications:

1. After you create a document in OpenOffice.org, choose File ➤ Save As. The window shown in Figure 5-8 opens.

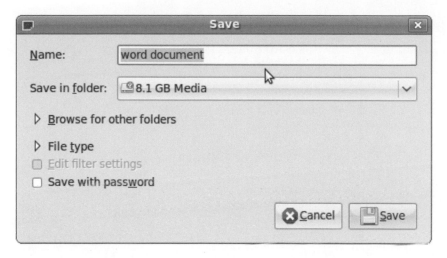

Figure 5-8. *Using the Save window, you can save a document in any of the supported document types.*

2. Click the "File type" option. Doing so displays a list of all supported file types. The following are those related to Microsoft Office:

- Office 2003XML

- Office 97/2000/XP (currently the most widely accepted)

- Office 95

- Office 6.0

3. Select the document type you want to use, and then click Save. Doing so writes the document in the specified format to your computer's hard disk. You'll see a warning, as shown in Figure 5-9, saying that you may lose certain formatting or content when saving in another format. Click Keep Current Format to save in the selected document format anyway.

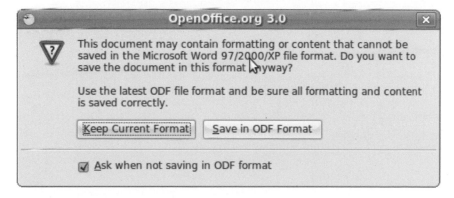

Figure 5-9. *Before you save in an alternative document format, you see a warning indicating that you may lose certain formatting or content.*

Permanently Changing the Document Type

The previous steps explained how to temporarily change the document type. If you use this technique, you'll need to do so again the next time you save a document. If you're constantly exchanging files with people who use Microsoft Office, you may want to change the default document type permanently. The following procedure describes how to do that:

1. In any OpenOffice.org application, choose Tools ➤ Options ➤ Load/Save ➤ General. Doing so opens the window shown in Figure 5-10.

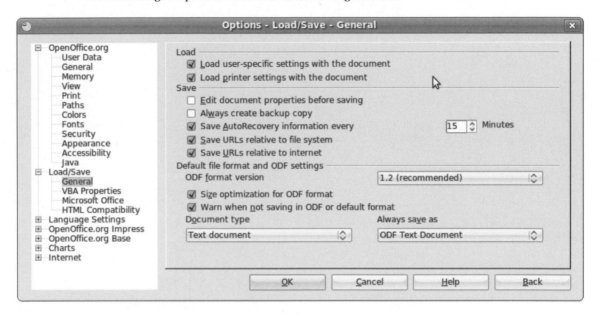

Figure 5-10. *To permanently change the default document type, work from the Load/Save option in the Tools ➤ Options menu.*

2. Set the file format for each of the document types you work with. To do this, make a selection from the Document Type drop-down list at lower-left. For instance, choose "Text document" to change the document type for documents you create using Writer.

3. Select the default document format from the "Always save as" drop-down list. For a text document, for instance, choose the Microsoft Word format to ensure maximum compatibility with Microsoft Office. For the best possible compatibility, select the Word 2003–compatible format.

4. Repeat this procedure for spreadsheets you create with Calc and presentations you make with Impress. Click OK to save and apply the changes.

Becoming Familiar with Specific OpenOffice.org Features

OpenOffice.org has some features that are specific to it and don't occur in other office suites. Among the most important of these is the option to work with extensions. Extensions offer additional functionality; they're used as extra programs that you install into OpenOffice.org. To install extensions, you use the Extension Manager located on the Tools menu of all the OpenOffice.org applications (see Figure 5-11).

Figure 5-11. To add functionality to OpenOffice.org, use the Extension Manager.

As you can see in Figure 5-11, by default only a limited number of extensions are listed. Click the "Get more extensions here" link in the lower-left corner to open the Firefox browser and go to the OpenOffice.org extensions home page (see Figure 5-12). You can also reach this page directly by starting your browser and entering the URL http://extensions.services.openoffice.org/getmore.

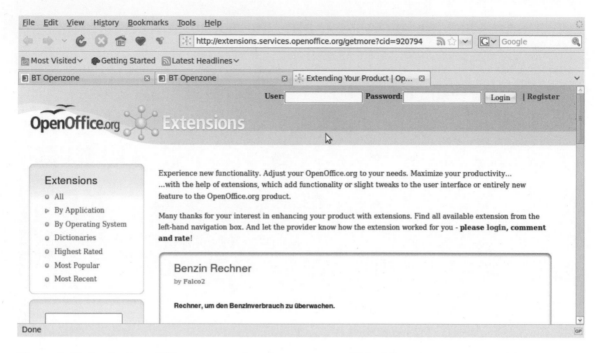

Figure 5-12. On the OpenOffice.org extensions home page, you'll find lots of extensions to add.

When you're working with the Extension Manager, make sure you're looking at extensions for the right operating system. To be sure you see Linux extensions only, click By Operating System in the Extensions list at left on the Extensions web page. Then, select Linux, and click Submit. You can also go through the list of most popular extensions. At the time I was writing this, the most popular extension was a French dictionary. Another extension that you'll probably find on the Most Popular list is the Sun PDF Import Extension; this is a module that imports and lets you edit DF files in OpenOffice.org Writer.

To install an extension, follow these steps:

1. Click the icon next to the extension's description. Doing so opens a window that gives you more information about the extension and shows a list of all operating systems for which the extension is available (see Figure 5-13).

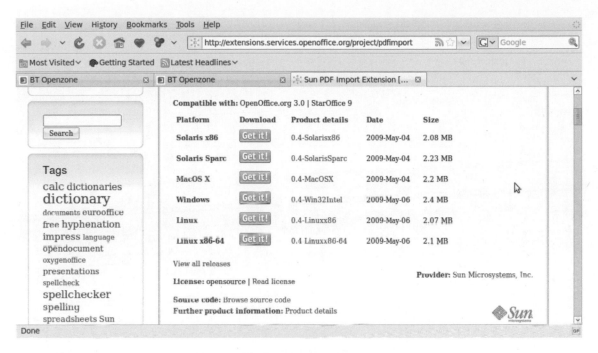

Figure 5-13. Some extensions are for specific operating systems only.

2. Click the "Get it!" icon next to Linux. Doing so starts the download automatically and opens the window shown in Figure 5-14. Select Save File, and click OK to save the extension to your desktop.

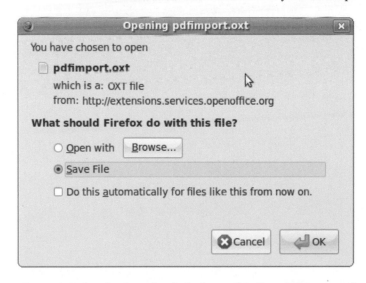

Figure 5-14. In the download window, select Save File to save the extension to your desktop.

3. After you download an extension, open the Ubuntu netbook main interface (see Figure 5-15) and click the Desktop icon in the upper-right corner.

Figure 5-15. Click the Desktop icon to browse to the items that have been placed on your desktop.

4. The File Browser opens and display the extension file. You can recognize it by the last part of the filename, which is most likely .oxt (see Figure 5-16).

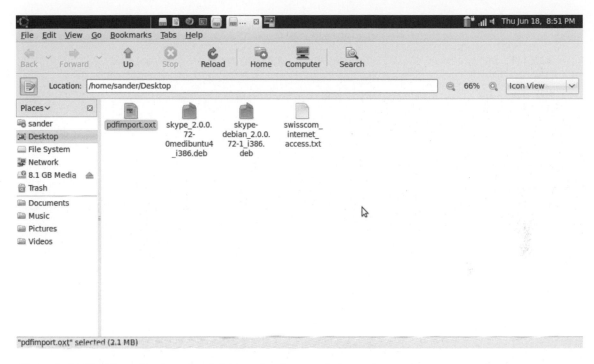

Figure 5-16. You'll see the downloaded extension in your desktop view.

5. Double-click the extension. Doing so opens the Extension Manager, which tells you that you're about to install the selected extension (see Figure 5-17). To start the installation, click OK.

Figure 5-17. Click OK to start the installation of the extension.

6. What happens now depends on the extension you're installing. To install the PDF Import module that I'm using in this example, you must scroll completely through the license agreement and click Accept (see Figure 5-18).

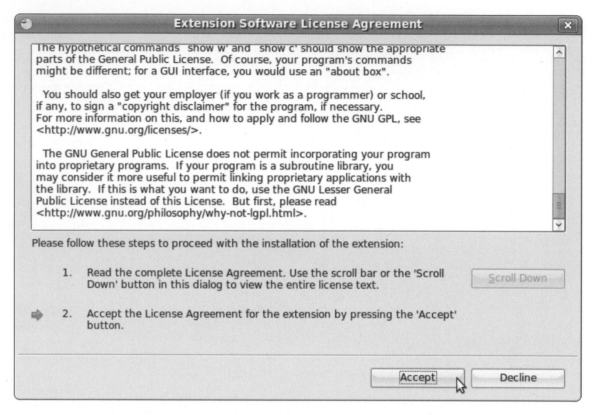

Figure 5-18. Click Accept to indicate that you're OK with the license agreement.

7. The extension is imported into OpenOffice.org. A description tells you what you can do with it. In the case of the PDF Import module, you can import a PDF and change small portions of it. (Be aware that the PDF Import module is far from perfect! The results may be disappointing, especially if the fonts used to create the PDF aren't installed on your computer—which is the case in most situations.) After you read the description, click Close to close the Extension Manager. In most cases, you'll find the functionality that has been added by the extension in the Tools menu of the OpenOffice.org application it applies to.

Working with OpenOffice.org Styles

One of the neatest features in OpenOffice.org is the ability to work with styles. You can set styles for characters, paragraphs, frames, pages, and lists. Most commonly, you'll work with paragraph styles in Writer documents; from time to time, you may use page styles.

   If you set up paragraph styles, you'll never again have to waste time fiddling with font settings on individual paragraphs and headings. You just select the text and set the style from the Style drop-down menu, and that's it. If you want to change the font size of, for example, all the body text in a document, you can edit the Text Body style once and the change is made throughout the document.

To bring up the Styles and Formatting window, press F11 (see Figure 5-19). Here, you can select the style you want to work with and apply it to your text. To do so, first double-click the style you want to use, and then enter your text. After you enter your text, you'll automatically return to the default Text Body style.

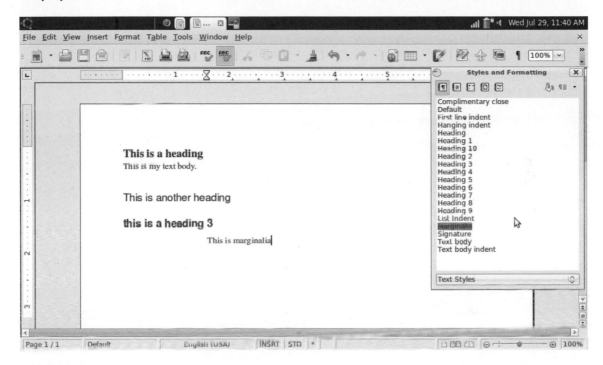

Figure 5-19. Using formatting styles makes it easy to create the appropriate layout for your documents.

A great side benefit of using styles is that it's easy to create a professional-looking table of contents. While working on your document, be sure to style you headings appropriately, using Heading 1, Heading 2, and so on. When you're finished, put your cursor where you want to create the table of contents. Next, choose Insert ➤ Indexes and Tables ➤ Indexes and Tables, and accept all the defaults; and click OK. A perfect table of contents will appear at the selected position.

You'll really find out why using styles is handy when you update a style's settings. If you change anything about the layout of selected text that has a style applied, you only have to update the style to apply the changes to all other items in the text that have the same style applied. The following example shows how to change the Heading style to use an italic font:

1. Open the Styles and Formatting window by pressing F11.

2. Double-click the Heading style to apply it to your text. Type the heading in your document, and then enter more text, including other headings.

3. Select one heading, and press Ctrl-I to make it italics.

4. In the Styles and Formatting window, from the drop-down menu at upper right (the downward-pointing triangle), select Update Style (see Figure 5-20).

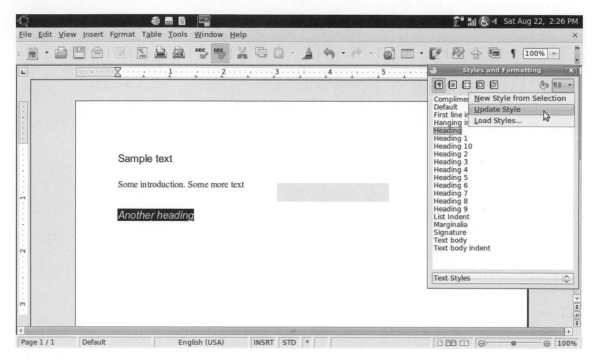

Figure 5-20. *Updating a style is as easy as selecting text.*

    5.   The new formatting is automatically applied to all text elements that have the same style applied.

After you get used to working with styles, you'll find that you have lots of options. For instance, you can save the formatting settings you've applied to selected text to a style, by selecting the text and then selecting the New Style from Selection option in the Styles and Formatting window (you can see this in Figure 5-20 as well). Doing so creates a new style that you can use in future documents.

Creating PDF Files

Among the strongest features of OpenOffice.org is the option to create PDF files from your documents without needing to purchase additional software. From any of the OpenOffice.org applications, you can access this option by choosing File ➤ Create PDF. This opens the PDF Options window shown in Figure 5-21.

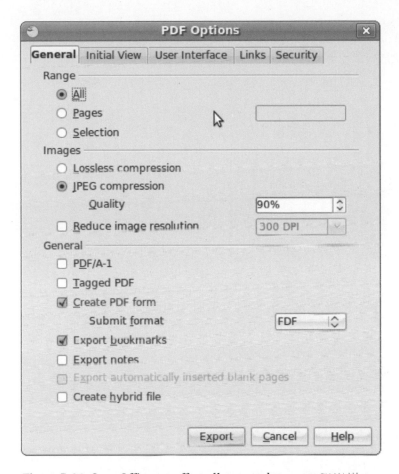

Figure 5-21. OpenOffice.org offers all you need to create PDF files.

On the General tab of the PDF Options window are some generic options, such as the type of PDF file you want to create, the quality you want to use, and the range of pages you want to include in the PDF file. After you specify these settings (in most cases, the defaults are fine), you can use the Initial View tab to define what the user sees when they open the PDF (see Figure 5-22).

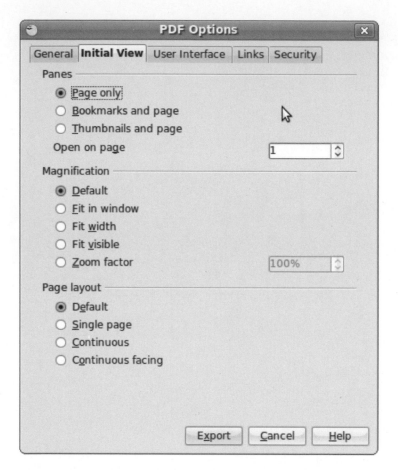

Figure 5-22. On the Initial View tab, you can specify what the user sees after opening the PDF.

By default, the user sees the text in the PDF you've created; but if you want to, you can show bookmarks and thumbnails in a sidebar. Also useful is the Magnification option, which helps you define how to display the document. For instance, if you want it to fit the width of the document at all times (which in very netbook friendly), select Fit in Window.

The options on the User Interface tab (see Figure 5-23) are related to the Initial View options. Whereas the Initial View options control the way the document is displayed, the options on the User Interface tab are associated with the program window. For instance, you can hide certain elements in the program interface; this makes reading text easier and is netbook friendly, because it lets you optimize the way you use your netbook's graphical display.

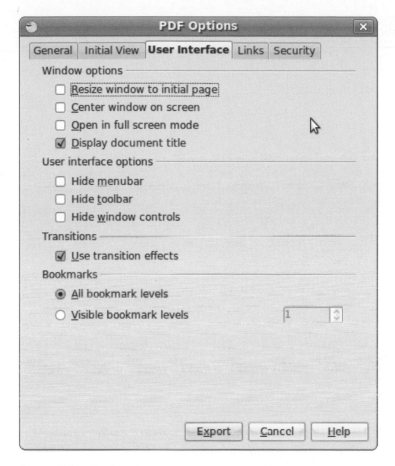

Figure 5-23. On the User Interface tab, you determine what the application looks like after you start it.

Relatively advanced options appear on the Links tab (see Figure 5-24). As the name suggests, these options allow you to refer to other documents. Using these options may be difficult, because they require that a specific document structure already be in place.

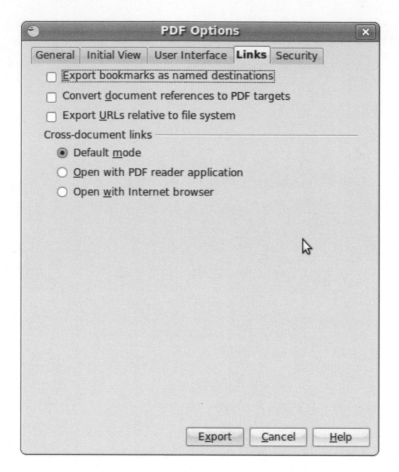

Figure 5-24. The Links options allow you to link to other PDF documents.

Last but not least, you can apply security settings to your PDFs. Using the options on the Security tab (see Figure 5-25), you can encrypt a document, or restrict printing or changing of the document. For instance, you can allow only low-resolution printing or not allow any changes. If you work with encryption or restrictions on your PDFs, you'll want to require a password. Users can then apply changes or decrypt the PDF only after they've entered the password.

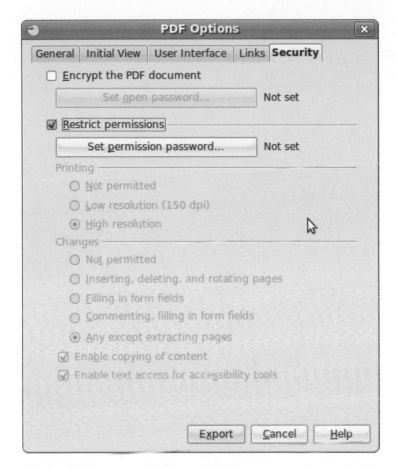

Figure 5 25. You can protect your PDF documents with passwords and encryption.

Additional Documentation

OpenOffice.org is a complex program, composed of millions of lines of code. I can only give you a brief introduction in this chapter. If you want to make the most of this powerful software, you can find out much more from the mass of tutorials and how-tos available online. A good starting point is Solveig Haugland's OpenOffice.org Training, Tips, and Ideas blog at http://www.openoffice.blogs.com. Apress also has a book titled *Beginning OpenOffice 3: From Novice to Professional* (http://www.apress.com/book/view/9781430215905).

Summary

In this chapter, you've learned about some of OpenOffice.org's strengths and particularities. If you've previously worked with an office suite, you'll find that it's not hard to change to OpenOffice.org. In the next chapter, you'll learn how to work with multimedia files in Ubuntu Netbook Remix.

■ ■ ■

CHAPTER 6

Working with Media

With Ubuntu on a netbook, you can fully enjoy your multimedia experience. There is one issue, though: for legal reasons, you won't find proprietary software packages and codecs that play back certain media types installed on Ubuntu Netbook Remix (other Ubuntu Netbook distributions, such as Easy Peasy, offer more possibilities). Hence, before you can fully enjoy Ubuntu Linux multimedia, you need to install some additional software. This chapter teaches you how to install this software and how to fully enjoy multimedia files on Ubuntu. This chapter covers the following topics:

- Enhancing Ubuntu Netbook Remix with restricted packages
- Watching movies on Ubuntu Netbook Remix
- Organizing and optimizing your digital picture collection
- Listening to audio

Enhancing Ubuntu Netbook Remix with Restricted Packages

Digital audio and video come wrapped up in a wide variety of formats. The most famous of these is the MP3 audio compression format. Although it's almost universally used, the MP3 format is subject to legal restrictions because several companies have successfully claimed that they hold patents covering the technology. Microsoft, Apple, and anyone else who wants to include the ability to play MP3s in their operating system have to pay massive licensing fees to the patent holders. The situation is similar for almost all of the commonly used formats for digital audio and video.

It would be impossible for projects such as Ubuntu, which distribute their software for free, to pay big bucks to patent holders. This is why, when you install Ubuntu, you'll find that it can play free, unpatented media formats such as Ogg Vorbis, but it can't play MP3 and other non-free formats. However, it's fairly easy to install the additional software you need to play the non-free formats.

Ubuntu offers a simple way of installing the most commonly needed non-free software, including Adobe Flash and Microsoft fonts as well as media codecs. You can do this by adding software from the Ubuntu Restricted Extras package, as explained in the next subsection of this chapter. An additional convenient method for accessing a large range of non-free software is offered by the Medibuntu project. Later, in the section "Installing Media Support Using the Medibuntu Repositories," you'll learn how to use it.

Some people prefer to use the Medibuntu repositories because Medibuntu includes more software than the Ubuntu Restricted Extras package. But I recommend that you use the Ubuntu Restricted Extras package, because it's on in the list of software that is maintained by Ubuntu and is therefore easier to support on your computer. Also, installing this package is much easier than installing the Medibuntu software. This section explains how to install both of them so that you can make your own choice.

Installing Ubuntu Restricted Extras for Media Support

As mentioned, using the Ubuntu Restricted Extras package is the best way to support restricted media files on your computer. This package provides support for MP3 playback, DVD file format playback, and more, such as Flash support. Chances are, you already installed this package while reading the "Working with Plugins, Add-ins, and Extensions" section in Chapter 4 of this book. If not, please refer back to that section.

Installing Media Support Using the Medibuntu Repositories

Before you begin to work with the Medibuntu repositories, you should know what sort of software they contain. They provide two types of software packages. The first kind are free as in *freedom* (open source) but legally problematic in some countries. This is the reason you won't ever find this software in the official Ubuntu repositories. You can install and use these packages, but doing so is completely at your own risk. (You shouldn't be worried when using the software described in this chapter—there have been no known cases in which a Linux user has been prosecuted for installing and using such software.)

The second kind of software in the Medibuntu repositories isn't distributed using an open source license. You're free to install the software components that fall into this category. The only reason a popular program like Skype, which lets you make free phone calls over the Internet, isn't included in the default Ubuntu Netbook Remix repositories is that it uses a license that isn't open source. Because this software has its own license, you need to download and install it directly from the website of the company that created it. Programs such as Skype, Adobe Reader, and Google Earth are made available from the Medibuntu repositories for your convenience.

■ **Note** The Evince software offers all you need to read PDF files. According to some people, it's not as good as Adobe Reader. So, you must make your own choice!

To install the Medibuntu software, you need to add the Medibuntu repositories. The following procedure shows how to do this:

1. From the Administration tab, start the Software Sources program. Enter your password to get access to the administration utility, shown in Figure 6-1.

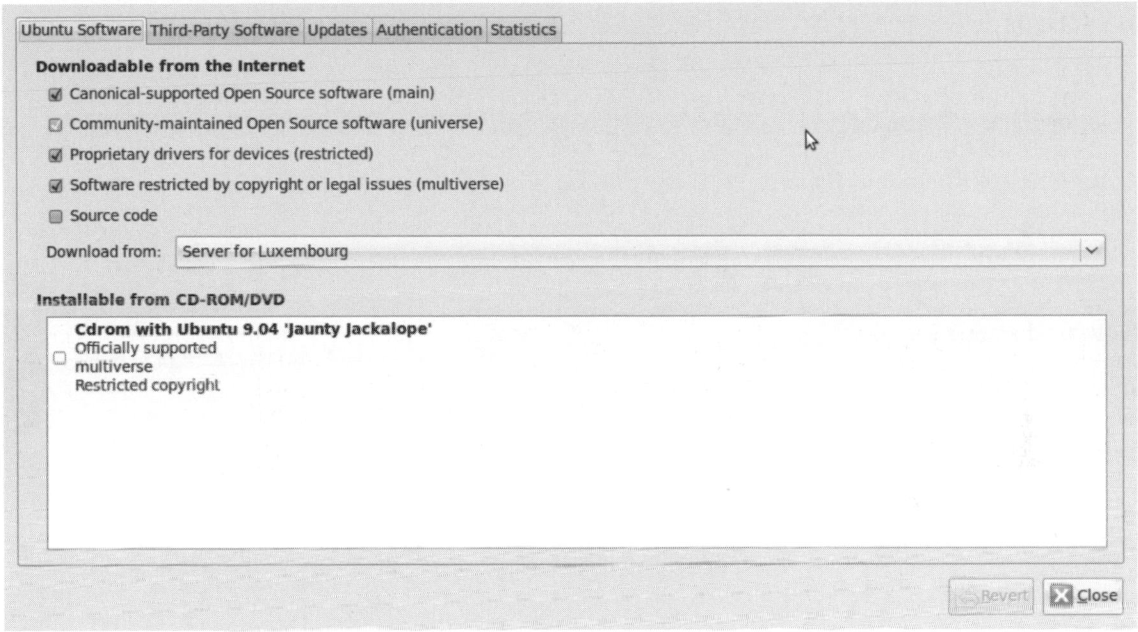

Ubuntu Software | Third-Party Software | Updates | Authentication | Statistics

Downloadable from the Internet

☑ Canonical-supported Open Source software (main)

☐ Community-maintained Open Source software (universe)

☑ Proprietary drivers for devices (restricted)

☑ Software restricted by copyright or legal issues (multiverse)

☐ Source code

Download from: | Server for Luxembourg | ⌄

Installable from CD-ROM/DVD

☐ **Cdrom with Ubuntu 9.04 'Jaunty Jackalope'**
Officially supported
multiverse
Restricted copyright

Revert ☒ Close

Figure 6-1. You need the Software Sources program to add additional sites for installation of software.

2. On the Third-Party Software tab, click Add to add a new resource. As you can see in Figure 6-2, this opens a window in which you can enter the complete path of the installation source you want to add. Make sure it reads as follows:

```
http://packages.medibuntu.org/jaunty
```

Edit Source ☒

Type: | Binary | ⌄

URI: | http://packages.medibuntu.org/ |

Distribution: | jaunty |

Components: | free non-free |

Comment: | |

☒ Cancel   ⏎ OK

Figure 6-2. Use the complete URI to identify the location where you want to download the Medibuntu software.

3.   Click OK. The Medibuntu repositories are added, and you can install the software from them.

Watching Movies

After you install the Win32 Codec pack as described earlier, there's a reasonable chance that you can watch movies on your netbook. A reasonable chance—no less, no more. Make sure the media file containing your film is available on your netbook, and open the File Browser to the film's location (see Figure 6-3). The following procedure describes how to play back the media file:

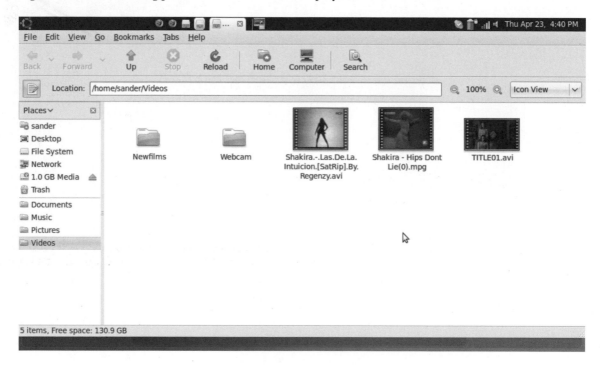

Figure 6-3. Open the File Browser so that you can access the folder containing your movie file.

1.   Double-click the media file to try to play it. If the media file was created with a supported codec, playback will start immediately. If no suitable codec was used, you're prompted to indicate whether you want to search for a suitable codec. If you want to play back the selected file, click Search to start searching.

2.   You see a list of all codecs that were found. To maximize the chances that you can play back your media file, select all of them, and click Install to install them. You have to confirm the installation of this software, to make sure you're aware of the fact that you may be installing software that is illegal in your country.

3. Installing new software packages requires administrator privileges, so you need to enter your password to give these permissions. Then, the software download will begin. It may take a few minutes. Following the download, the codec is installed automatically, and you return to the media player. If all is well, the movie begins playing (see Figure 6-4). Enjoy!

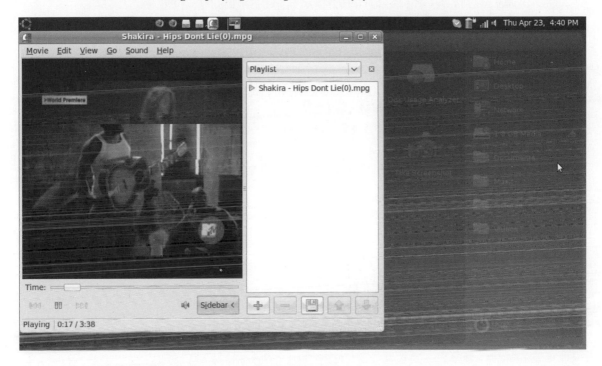

Figure 6-4. If all went well, you can now start watching the movie.

Working with Digital Pictures

Before you start copying your digital photos to your netbook, you should monitor the available disk space. To do this, start the File Browser by clicking the home folder in the launcher. The amount of free space is shown at lower left in the File Browser. Disk space is limited on some netbook computers; if your netbook is equipped with only a few gigabytes of flash memory, be careful, because copying your digital pictures over may fill the available memory rapidly.

If you have enough disk space, the F-Spot photo manager lets you manage your pictures. It offers some limited optimization possibilities as well. You can find F-Spot in the Graphics menu.

Importing Pictures into F-Spot

By default, as you can see in Figure 6-5, F-Spot shows an empty window. To do something useful, you have to first import photos. Before doing that, you must decide which options you want to use:

- *Detect duplicates:* This option tells F-Spot to look for duplicate pictures. Make sure this option is always selected; it makes sure photos that are detected twice are imported only once into F-Spot.

- *Copy files to the Photos folder:* This option is useful if you're importing photos from a digital camera. The photos are copied to the Photos folder that is managed by F-Spot. If you already have your photos on local storage, you should deselect this option. In that case, it would be a waste of disk space to copy them again to another directory on your local hard drive.

- *Include subfolders:* Select this option to make sure photos from subfolders are included.

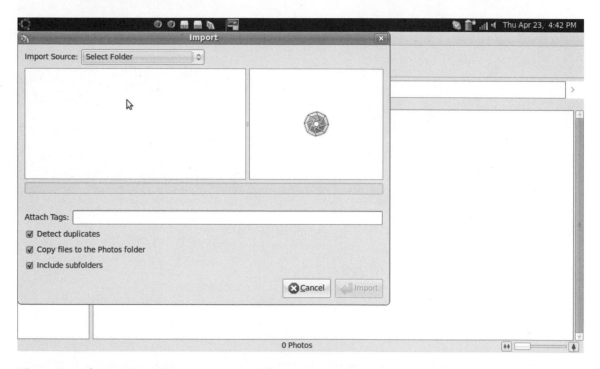

Figure 6-5. *After starting F-Spot, you must import your pictures.*

After you select the options you want to use, click Select Folder to browse to the location where your photos are stored. If a digital camera is attached, you'll see it, and you can browse directly to the folder on the camera where the pictures are stored. If this isn't the case, a File Browser window opens. From here, you can browse to the folder that contains your pictures (see Figure 6-6).

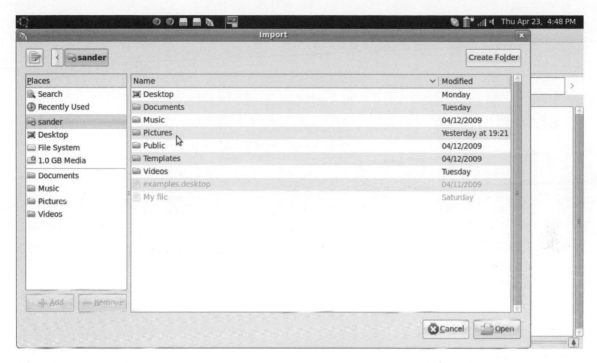

Figure 6-6. *Browse to the folder that contains your digital pictures.*

After selecting the folder that contains your pictures, click Open to open it. Doing so imports all pictures into F-Spot. Depending on the number of pictures you selected, this may take a while (see Figure 6-7).

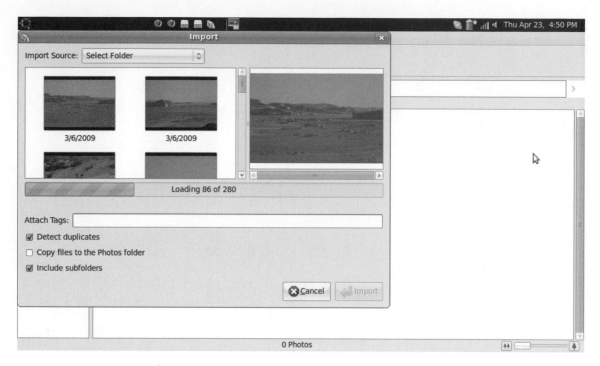

Figure 6-7. *It may take a while before all pictures are imported into F-Spot.*

Click the Import button shown in Figure 6-7 to bring all the pictures to the F-Spot main window, shown in Figure 6-8. In this window, you perform all photo-management tasks.

Figure 6-8. You perform all photo-management tasks in the F-Spot main window.

Organizing Your Pictures

The goal of F-Spot is threefold: you use it to organize, optimize, and display images. To do your work efficiently, it's important that you select the right perspective first. You can do that using the button bar at the top of the window. Click the Browse button for a thumbnail overview of all your pictures. If you want to edit a specific picture, you can use the Edit Image button to open it in an editor.

You'll also see that the context changes with the function you choose. When you're in the Browse view, you can add tags to pictures, and you see a summary of information about the pictures. In Edit Image view, you see more details about the selected picture as well as some options that help you optimize the picture (see Figure 6-9).

Figure 6-9. In the Edit Image perspective, you have direct access to options to optimize your pictures.

Before you begin to optimize your pictures, it's a good idea to organize them. Among the first actions you may want to perform is tagging the pictures. Five tags are available by default: Favorites, Hidden, People, Places, and Events. You can drag a tag to a photo or to a selection of photos (use Ctrl-click to make your selection).

After you've properly marked all your pictures with tags, it's not hard to find all those in the same category. To do so, select Find ➤ Find Selected Tag, and select a tag; you then see all pictures that have this tag applied (see Figure 6-10). After locating all photos that have the same tag attached, you can drag the tag away from the brown bar above the thumbnails toolbar to return to the overview of all your pictures.

Figure 6-10. You can easily find all photos from the same category by using the Find ➤ Find Selected Tag option.

If you think you have to make do with the default tags, you're wrong. Right-click in the part of the screen where you see all the current tags, and from the menu select Create New Tag. Next, specify a parent tag if you want to use one. For instance, if you've been on a holiday in Iceland, it makes sense to create a subtag with the name Iceland under the parent tag Places. But you don't have to use a parent tag; in that case, select (None) as the parent tag. Then, type the name of the new tag you want to create, and click Create (see Figure 6-11).

Figure 6-11. When creating new tags, it makes sense to place them under a common parent tag.

When you create a new tag, it's placed as a new item under the parent tag. It doesn't get an icon by default; the icon used for that tag is the first picture for which you use the tag, so you should choose a nice photo! If your pictures are too small for you to choose a nice picture to use for your tag, drag the slide bar at lower right. Dragging it to the right zooms in on the thumbnails. This lets you take a better look at them (see Figure 6-12).

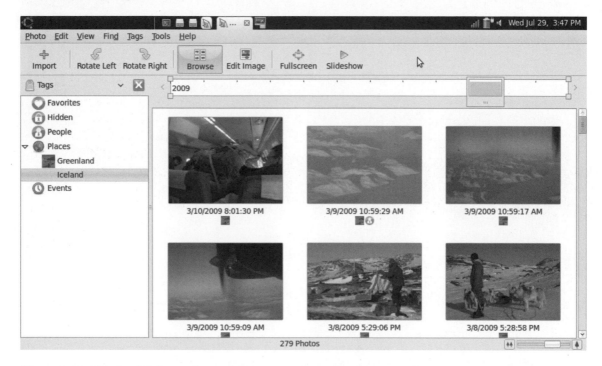

Figure 6-12. Use the slide bar at lower right to zoom in on the photo overview.

■ **Tip** Tagging a picture is easy, and removing the tag is almost as easy. Just right-click the picture, and select the option Remove Tag. If the selected picture has multiple tags, on the submenu you can indicate which tag you want to remove.

The screen of a netbook computer normally isn't very large, so you may also want to work in fullscreen view when you tag your pictures. This is how it works:

1. Select the first photo you want to work on in fullscreen view.

2. On the toolbar, click the Fullscreen button. Use the arrow keys to view the photos one by one.

3. When you're ready to tag a picture, right-click it, and select Attach Tag from the menu. Then, choose the tag that you want to add to the selected picture.

4. Use the arrow keys to browse to the next picture, and repeat this procedure (see Figure 6-13).

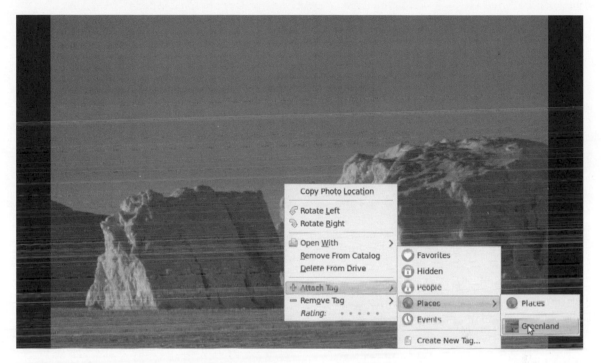

Figure 6-13. If you don't see enough in Browse mode, use fullscreen view to tag your pictures.

Another way to organize your photos is by rating them. This also isn't hard to do. Right-click the photo you want to rate; the last option in the menu is the Rating option. By default, five dots are shown. You can indicate your appreciation of the photo by clicking one of the dots. If you click the leftmost dot, you make this a one-star picture. If you click the rightmost dot, you mark it as a five-star photo. You can rate individual photos; or you can select multiple photos, right-click the selection, and rate them all at once (see Figure 6-14).

Figure 6-14. *You can rate photos to make it easier to find back your most beautiful pictures.*

When you're finished tagging and rating your pictures, you can use the options from the Find menu to find them. This menu contains options to find pictures by tag, by rating, or by using a combination of multiple criteria. For instance, locate all photos tagged with People. Next, choose Find ➤ By Rating ➤ Set Rating filter to create a rating filter; use five stars as both the Min Rating and as the Max Rating. These options show you only five-star People pictures (see Figure 6-15). Don't forget to clear the rating filter to see all your pictures again.

Figure 6-15. To make sure you see only your most beautiful pictures, you can set a rating filter and combine that with specific tags.

Enhancing Your Pictures

Now that you've organized your pictures so that you can easily find the ones you're looking for, you can enhance them. That means you can remove small irregularities from the photos and apply other kinds of corrections. To do so, start by double-clicking the picture you want to optimize. This opens the window shown in Figure 6-16.

Figure 6-16. Double-click the picture you want to optimize.

At left in the Edit Image window, you can see all the different editing options. However, you can't clearly see which options are available, because the Histogram and Image Information windows are open as well. It's a good idea to close these; to do so, click the downward-pointing triangle to the left of the window name. Next, remove the brown search bar above your picture, by clicking the X at the right end of the bar (or clicking the refresh icon). To bring it back later, press Ctrl+F. If you still can't see enough, you can remove other screen elements as well. To do so, look at the options on the View menu. For instance, by removing the toolbar, you gain a few more valuable centimeters to see your pictures; you can also remove the filmstrip from the screen. All of these elements are easy to put back later if you need them. You now have a somewhat better view of the available editing options; make sure your computer screen looks like Figure 6-17 before continuing.

Figure 6-17. *Before starting to edit your photos, it's a good idea to remove some unneccessary elements from the screen.*

Now that you've cleaned up your display, it's time to begin editing and optimizing. First, you can add comments to your photos. To do this, type whatever you want in the Comment bar below the photo. And did you notice that in this view you can also rate the picture? Use the five dots to the right of the Comment bar.

Next, you can zoom in on your picture using the loupe tool. To enable it, select View ➤ Loupe (or press the letter *v* on your keyboard). You now see a magnifying glass that lets you zoom in on certain parts of the picture so you can better see what it shows (see Figure 6-18). Just click on the magnifying glass and drag it around. When you place the small circle over an area of the photo, an enlarged view is shown in the big circle. To switch off the loupe, select View ➤ Loupe again (or press *v*), and it will disappear.

Figure 6-18. Use the loupe tool to zoom in on certain parts of your photo.

The loupe isn't the only tool available to zoom in on pictures. At lower right on the screen is the zoom tool; you can drag the bar to the right to zoom in. This gives you a level of detail that lets you almost work on a pixel level.

Now, let's look at the different menu options that are available to edit your pictures. First, you may want to crop a photo. Let's face it—when you take a picture, there's often a little too much information, which you may want to remove. To crop, first drag the mouse over the picture to make a selection. You can adjust the dimensions of the selection by hovering the mouse over the corners or sides and then clicking and dragging. You can move the entire selection by clicking and dragging it. Click Crop to crop the picture to your selection.

If you need a specific format while cropping the picture, first click the Crop button. Doing so displays a drop-down menu from which you can choose a crop ratio (see Figure 6-19). Next, click and drag on the picture as you did for an unconstrained crop selection. The selection is constrained to your chosen ratio. When you click the Crop button, you automatically return to the main menu. Don't like the result? No worries—select Photo ➤ Version ➤ Original to return to the original version.

■ **Tip** F-Spot never changes the originals of your pictures. Whatever happens, you can always get back to the original using Photo ➤ Version ➤ Original.

Figure 6-19. Select a constraint, and then drag the mouse over the picture to crop it.

The next useful function is red-eye reduction. This feature is easy to use. Select Red-eye Reduction, use the mouse to select the area that contains the eyes you want to fix in the picture, and then click Fix. F-Spot automatically analyzes your photo and tries to make it as good as it can.

Another function that offers few options is Desaturate. It removes all the color from your picture. The same is true for the Sepia option, which changes the colors in the picture to sepia tones.

The Straighten option lets you interact with the program. It lets you correct a photo if you didn't held your camera completely straight (you'll notice that this is the case for a lot of pictures!). To correct this issue, drag the slide bar under Straighten until the picture is exactly the way you want it to be (see Figure 6-20).

Figure 6-20. *Use the Straighten function to correct the horizon in your pictures.*

If you want the area around the central subject of your picture to disappear in a blur, you can use the Soft Focus option (see Figure 6-21). This option also uses a slide bar. Here's my personal advice: don't use it this option. It's ugly in most situations. But you may like it if you want to make romantic photos, for instance. People who know how to handle this function can do nice things with it.

Figure 6-21. The Soft Focus option doesn't always improve the quality of your pictures.

The Auto Color option can be very useful. This option can bring color to your pictures; but if it doesn't understand the white balance, it's capable of messing up your photos as well. Try it; and if you don't like it, you can use Photo ➤ Version ➤ Original to return to the original version of your picture

Last but not least is the Adjust Color option. This isn't just an option—It gives you access to slide bars that let you correct your picture in many ways (see Figure 6-22). You can change basically everything from here. My advice is to try things and see whether you like the changes. Like what you see? Keep it that way. Don't like it? Revert back to the default setting, which is 0 in most cases.

Figure 6-22. Under the Adjust Color option are options that let you change many aspects of your photos.

Your pictures should now look good and be organized. It's time to proceed to the last part of your Ubuntu netbook multimedia experience: listening to some music.

Enjoying Your Music

From time to time, you may want to listen to music. Using an Ubuntu netbook, two approaches are available. First, you can listen to digital music files that are stored on your computer. Second, you may be interested in connecting your portable audio player to your Ubuntu netbook.

Playing Back Audio Files

It doesn't matter if you want to play back audio files on your computer's hard drive or connect your iPod—with Rhythmbox music player, you can do it all. Before you play any media files however, you need to import them into the player. The following procedure explains how to do that:

1. From the Sound & Video menu, click Rhythmbox. Doing so opens the program, as shown in Figure 6-23.

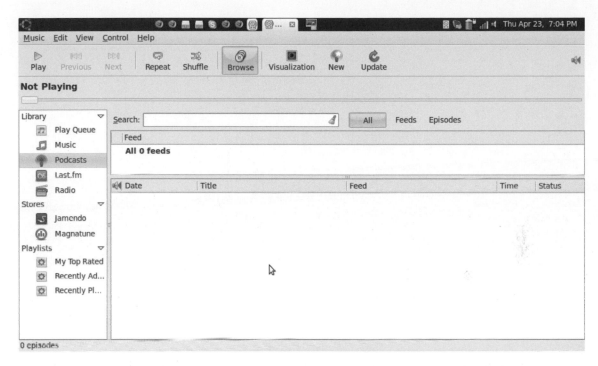

Figure 6-23. Rhythmbox offers a universal solution to play all kinds of audio.

2. You need to import your music files. There are different options to do that, all of which are available from the Music menu. To import individual files, use the Import File option. To get complete folders that contain music files, use the Import Folder option. And if your music is on some kind of removable media such as a USB flash drive or SD card, use the Scan Removable Media option. Let's assume you want to import an individual music file; select Music ➤ Import File.

3. You see a File Browser window in which you can browse to the folder that contains your music files. Select the file you want to import, and click Open to import it into your computer (see Figure 6-24).

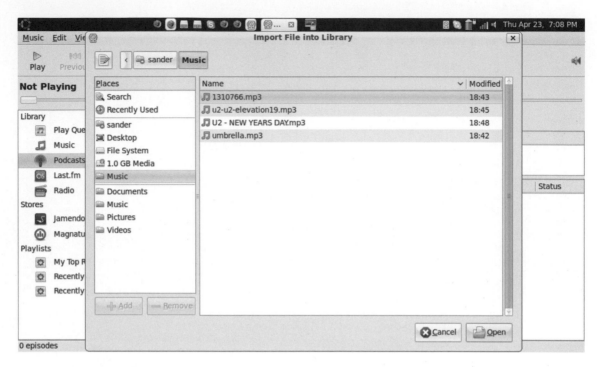

Figure 6-24. Select a file, and click Open to import it into the Music library.

4. When you've finished importing music files, they appear under the Music option (see Figure 6-25). From there, you can play them.

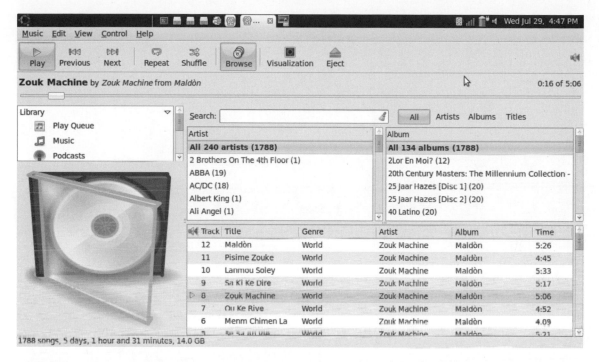

Figure 6-25. From the Music library, you can play your music files.

That wasn't hard, was it? Rhythmbox can import complete folders as well. The procedure is similar to the one for importing files, but you select Music ➤ Import Folder (or use the shortcut Ctrl-O). Now, browse to the folder, and select it. Click OK to load it into Rhythmbox.

In most cases, this procedure works well. But you may encounter a situation where the file you're trying to import isn't supported. In that case, a pop-up opens, telling you that the file type is unsupported and Ubuntu needs to locate a suitable codec. Follow the prompts that are presented to install the codec, and your media file will be playing within a couple of minutes.

The iPod and Other Portable Audio Players

Generic portable media players show up on your netbook as ordinary USB mass storage devices, just like a flash drive. When you connect your player to the netbook, a File Browser window pops up, showing its contents. You can drag songs over from your Music folder to copy them onto your player. When you're finished, close the File Browser window, right-click the icon on the desktop that represents your player, and choose "Unmount volume" before unplugging the device. If you're using an iPod, the situation is different.

The process to begin using an iPod isn't difficult. Connect it to your computer, and the netbook will detect that a new device has been connected. In a pop-up, you're asked what you want to do (see Figure 6-26). As you can see, the default action is to launch the default media player application, which in this case is Rhythmbox.

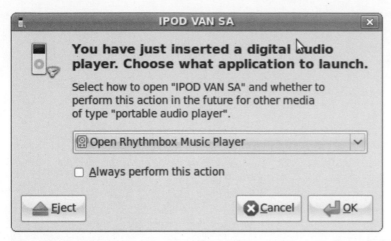

Figure 6-26. When you connect an iPod, Ubuntu proposes to launch the default media player.

In Rhythmbox, Ubuntu shows the contents of the iPod. You'll see some differences compared to the contents shown on a computer that has iTunes. For instance, only custom playlists appear; the intelligent playlists managed by iTunes aren't shown. You can manage the music tracks on your iPod using Rhythmbox, just as you're used to managing music on any other media player. Figure 6-27 shows Rhythmbox after you connected your iPod to your netbook.

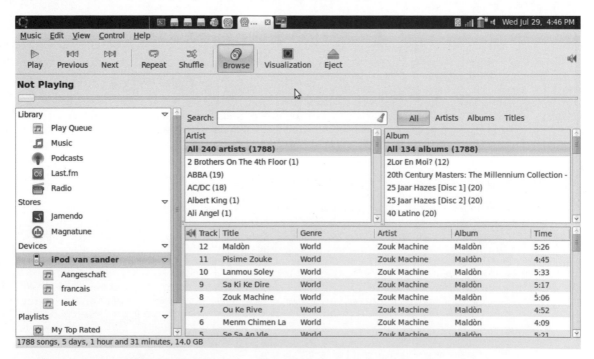

Figure 6-27. It's no problem for Rhythmbox to connect to your iPod.

Summary

In this chapter, you've learned how to work with different kinds of media files in Ubuntu Netbook Remix. You're now able to watch movie files, listen to music, copy music to your MP3 player, and organize and optimize digital pictures. In the next chapter, you'll learn how to change and optimize settings for your Ubuntu netbook computer.

CHAPTER 7

■ ■ ■

Optimizing Netbook Settings

When you're working with your netbook, it's handy to be able to optimize its settings and programs to match the way you prefer to work. In this chapter, you'll learn how to do that. If there's anything about the default behavior of your netbook that you don't like, after reading this chapter you'll know how to change it. The following topics are covered:

- Keyboard settings and shortcuts
- Configuring accessibility options
- Power management settings
- Tuning the display's efficiency

Keyboard Settings and Shortcuts

You'll find all the relevant configuration settings on the Preferences tab. Among them is the Keyboard program, which you can use to manage keyboard settings (see Figure 7-1). Using the options in this window, you can configure different aspects of your keyboard's behavior, as well as mouse settings.

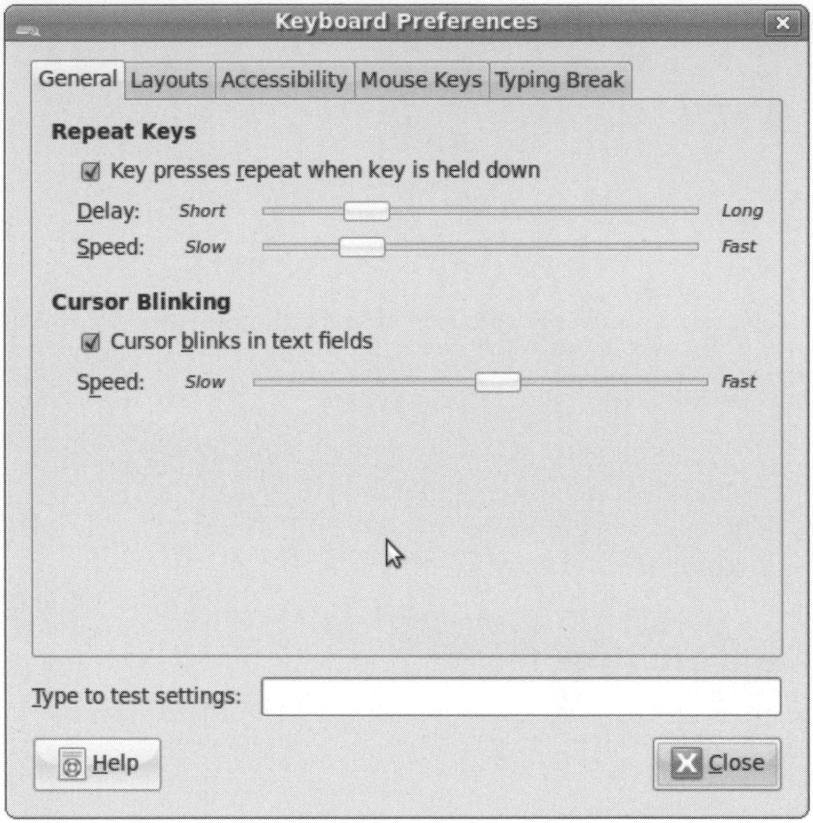

Figure 7-1. The Keyboard Preferences window provides options to configure keyboard settings.

On the General tab, shown in Figure 7-1, you can configure repeating keys and the cursor's blinking. These features are helpful if you don't like your keyboard's reaction speed. Under Repeat Keys are two options. First, you can use the Delay setting to determine how long to wait after you press and hold a key, before the key starts repeating itself. The Speed option indicates how quickly the key is repeated. Be sure neither option is set too far to the left, because that can be annoying. You don't want a character to appear four times if you only type it once, do you?

The Cursor Blinking option isn't as useful. It indicates how often the cursor blinks in a text interface such as OpenOffice.org Writer. If you want the cursor to blink a lot, drag the slide bar to the right; if you don't like the cursor to blink quickly, drag the slide bar to the left. (I can't imagine why you would care!)

After changing your settings, use the "Type to test settings" field at the bottom of the screen to find out whether the settings you've selected do what you need.

On the Layouts tab of the Keyboard Preferences window, you can change the keyboard layout used by Ubuntu. Normally, this should be set correctly during installation; but if you don't see the correct settings, or if you need more than one keyboard layout on your laptop, you can use the Add button to first add a new keyboard model and then select it from the list of selected layouts (see Figure 7-2). You can choose the layout you want to use by selecting the country, as well as by selecting a language (see Figure 7-3). Don't forget to use the "Type to test settings" field to be sure it's the correct layout for you.

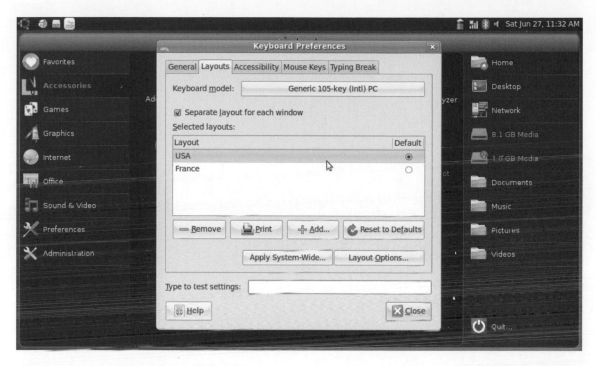

Figure 7-2. *If your default keyboard layout doesn't fit your needs, add a new layout and make it the default setting.*

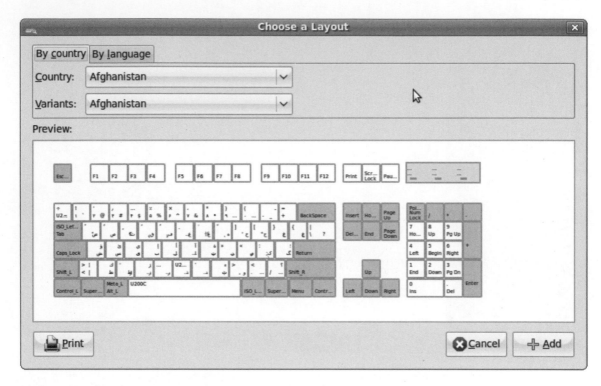

Figure 7-3. Select the keyboard you want to use by country or by specific language.

Also on the Layouts tab, you'll find the Layout Options button. Click it for more specific keyboard-related functions. In this window (see Figure 7-4), you can, for instance, determine which function is assigned to the Alt key, or whether a Euro sign should be added to one of the keys. These options give you flexibility to use your computer in specific settings, but you should also realize that some options make sense in specific international environments only. You wouldn't use the Japanese keyboard options if you're from Belgium, right?

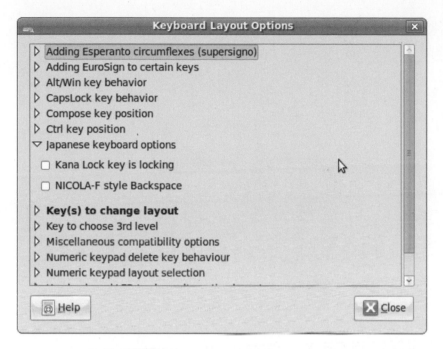

Figure 7-4. More specific options are available from the Keyboard Layout Options window.

Power-Management Settings

You probably bought your netbook for its portability, right? That means you want its battery to last as long as possible. Ubuntu Netbook Remix offers some options to increase battery life beyond the default.

Before you make any changes, look at the currently remaining battery life. You can do that by moving your mouse cursor over the battery power option in the upper-right corner of the screen (see Figure 7-5)

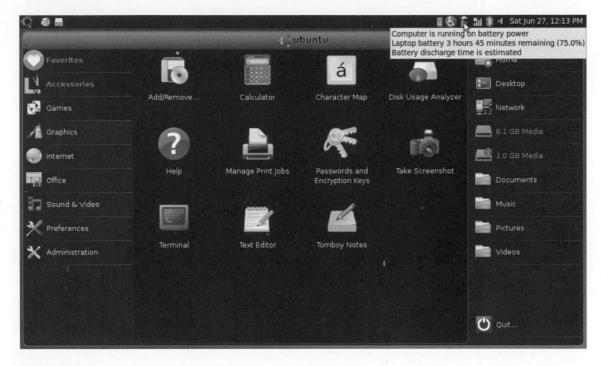

Figure 7-5. *Move the cursor over the battery icon to see how much power remains in your computer's battery.*

Clicking this button gives you access to three options:

- *Laptop battery:* This option shows information about the battery power remaining. The very useful window provides detailed device information, including the total charge time your battery needs, the time it takes to discharge completely and—very important—the current capacity. As you can see in Figure 7-6, the capacity of my netbook's battery is 97%, which is good. The lower it gets, the faster your battery will empty. Check this option from time to time to find out if it's time to buy a new battery.

■ **Note** I've seen some models whose battery capacity indicator is low but whose battery still functions well. Capacity is a good indicator, but don't rely on it too much.

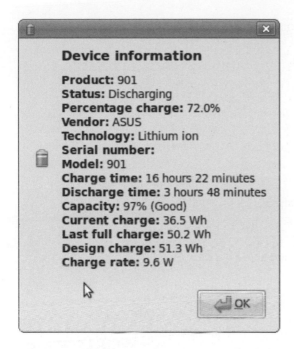

Device information

Product: 901
Status: Discharging
Percentage charge: 72.0%
Vendor: ASUS
Technology: Lithium ion
Serial number:
Model: 901
Charge time: 16 hours 22 minutes
Discharge time: 3 hours 48 minutes
Capacity: 97% (Good)
Current charge: 36.5 Wh
Last full charge: 50.2 Wh
Design charge: 51.3 Wh
Charge rate: 9.6 W

OK

Figure 7-6. The Device Information window provides useful information, including your battery's current capacity.

- *Suspend:* Use this option to suspend your computer. *Suspending* means the current state is written to memory, and your computer uses a minimal amount of battery power to maintain that state in memory. Suspending your computer is a good idea if you plan to using it again within minutes—for instance, when you're changing trains at a railway station. Be aware, however, that your battery will continue to be drained a little while suspended; if you leave the computer in suspended mode for hours, you'll most likely return to a completely empty battery. Use this option if you want to be capable of resuming your work as quickly as possible.

- *Hibernate:* Use this option to put your computer into hibernation. That means the current state of your computer is written to the computer's hard drive. In this state, the computer uses no power at all, but resuming your work will take more time. This option is excellent if you want to continue your work after an extended period. Note that on some models, Ubuntu doesn't support suspending well. Try this feature to be sure it works before you put your computer into what you assume is hibernation mode, put in your bag, and find out a few hours later that it didn't hibernate and has gotten much too hot.

■ **Tip** Even if your netbook doesn't support suspending or hibernation well, don't worry. Just shut it off—Ubuntu boots quickly, so you won't have to wait long.

If you want to set current power-management options, right-click the battery icon. Doing so gives you four options:

■ **Tip** If you won't be using certain features of the netbook's hardware for a session, you can save a lot of power by disabling them in the BIOS setup. After all, hardware devices consume a lot of power. To do so, press F2 or Del on boot (depending on the model you're using), find the section for onboard device configuration, and temporarily disable the devices you aren't using, such as wireless, LAN, audio, camera, speaker, and card reader. If you switch off the devices you're not using, your battery will last a lot longer. Owners of Asus Eee PC netbooks can install a handy third-party package called EeeControl, which lets you disable your camera, wireless, and card reader from a panel widget. You can even put your CPU into a special power-saving mode with a couple of clicks.

- *Preferences:* This option gives you access to different power-management preferences. In the next subsection, you'll read about the possibilities.

- *Power History:* When you use this option, you see a graph that shows the power usage on your computer since you last started it (see Figure 7-7). Useful to see what has happened at certain specific moments, but there is nothing to be optimized or changed here.

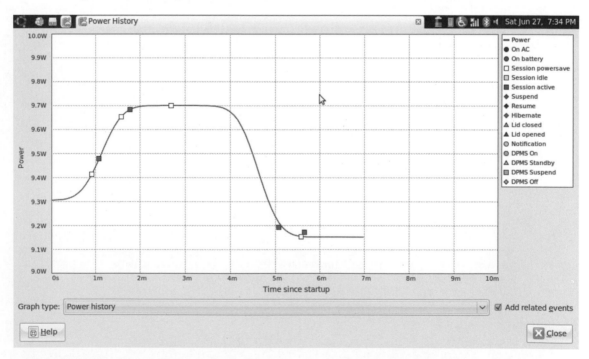

Figure 7-7. The Power History graph shows you how much power your computer has used since you last booted it.

- *Help:* This option gives you access to the GNOME Power Manager Manual, which explains everything about the power-management options.

- *About:* Look here to get information about the people who programmed the power-management interface.

Choosing More Efficient Power-Management Options

Ubuntu Netbook Remix offers you some options to optimize power usage on your netbook. You can access these options from the Power Management Preferences window that opens when you right-click the battery icon at upper right on your screen and choose Preferences. As you can see in Figure 7-8, the options are offered on three tabs.

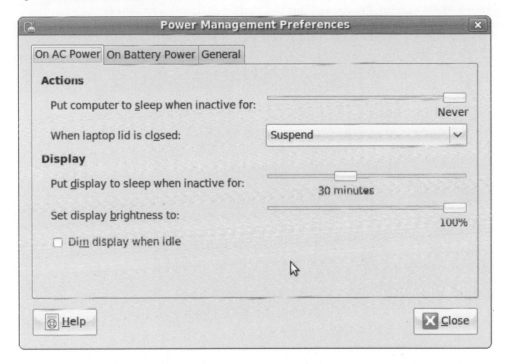

Figure 7-8. The Power Management Preferences window lets you optimize power usage on your computer.

On the On AC Power tab of the Power Management Preferences window, you can optimize your computer's power usage. These options apply only if your computer is connected to the electric grid; you don't need these options if your computer is on battery power. Under Actions, you can specify when your computer should be put to sleep. The default setting is Never, which makes sense if you netbook is plugged in. To be more energy efficient, you can set this to, for example, one hour, which will suspend your computer when you're away.

Next, you can specify what should happen when the lid of your netbook is closed. The default action is to suspend your current session to RAM. This is useful, but make sure it works before you relying on it. Alternatively, you can have your netbook do nothing or hibernate if you close the lid.

The second set of options relate to the graphical display. By default, your display goes to sleep after 30 minutes of inactivity, which in most cases is reasonable. To continue working, press any key, and the display will wake up. You can also set the display brightness. By default, it's as bright as possible. If you don't like that, use the slide bar to diminish the brightness setting. If you want to be more energy efficient, select the "Dim display when idle" option. Doing so will lower the display's brightness when you're inactive.

The options on the On Battery Power tab (see Figure 7-9) are similar to the options on the On AC Power tab, and apply when your computer is on battery power only. In most cases, you'll want to configure the settings more tightly on this tab, to use your computer's battery power as efficiently as possible. In addition to the settings from the On AC Power tab, two options are added. First is the option "When battery power is critically low." This defines what should happen when your battery has almost completely run down. The default action is to suspend the computer. You may want to hibernate the computer instead, because the computer doesn't use any energy when it's in hibernation mode. Next, under Display, is the "Reduce backlight brightness" option. You won't appreciate this option when you're working in full sunlight, but it lets you use your computer's battery power more efficiently. Make sure it's switched off if you're planning to do some work in the park on a sunny spring day; but in all other cases, leave it on.

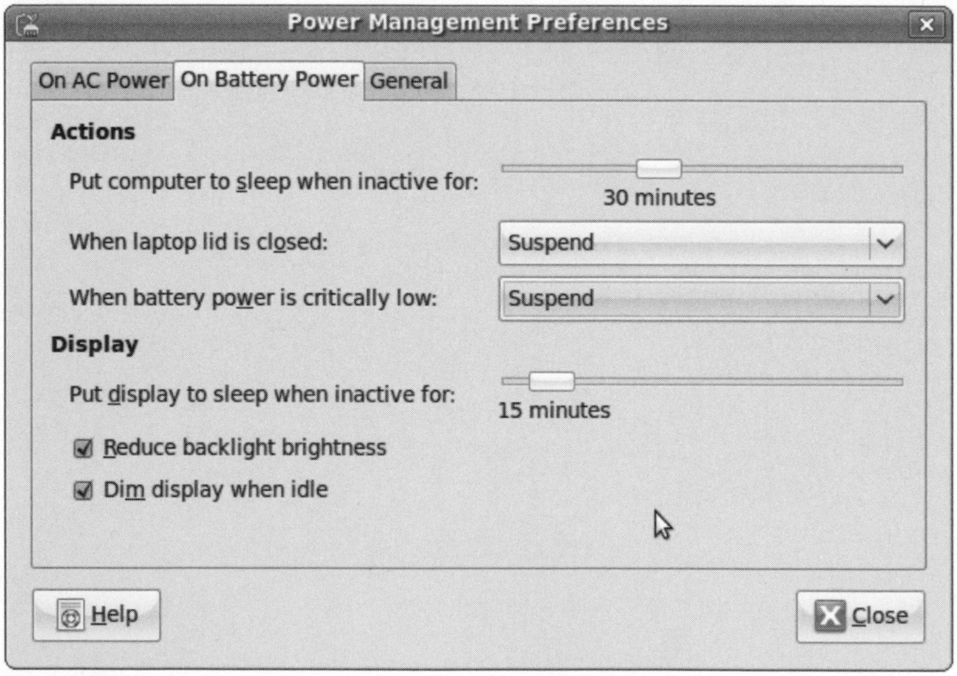

Figure 7-9. *The On Battery Power tab provides additional options that are specific to being on battery power only.*

Last, the General tab provides some generic options that are effective whether you're on AC power or on battery power (see Figure 7-10). First, under Actions, you can define what should happen when the power button or the suspend button is pressed. For both, you can choose from the following:

- Ask me

- Suspend

- Hibernate

- Shutdown

Choose the option that suits you best. Next are the Notification Area options, which let you specify when to show the battery icon. The default action is to always show this icon (which is a good idea), but you may choose one of the following three options:

- Only display an icon when battery power is critically low

- Only display an icon when charging or discharging

- Only display an icon when a battery is present.

Finally, you can enable the option to use a sound to notify you if there is an error condition, such as when the battery is critically low.

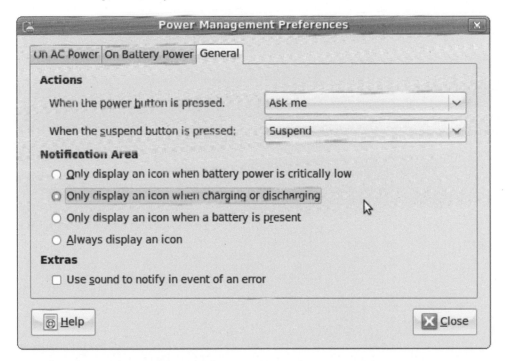

Figure 7-10. The most important options on the General tab let you define what should happen if you press the power or suspend button.

Configuring Accessibility Options

If you have mobility impairments or other physical issues that make using a conventionally configured computer difficult, you can refer to the Assistive Technologies option from the Preferences menu (see Figure 7-11). This window gives you access to four categories of options:

- *Preferred Applications:* You can set up a screen reader, a screen magnifier, and predictive text entry.

- *Keyboard Accessibility:* The items from this category make working with the keyboard easier for persons with physical issues that make working with a keyboard hard.

- *Accessible Login:* These options makes logging in easier for disabled persons.

- *Mouse Accessibility:* These options are specific to mouse usage.

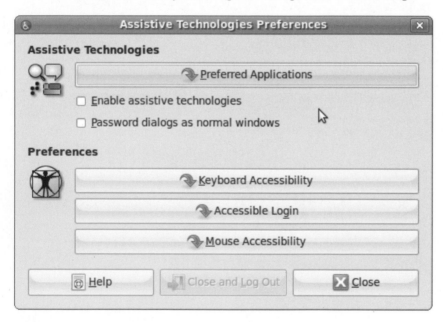

Figure 7-11. *The Assistive Technologies Preferences window is a convenient interface to various settings that can make your netbook easier to use if you have a mobility or visual impairment.*

Selecting Preferred Applications

The Preferred Applications button opens the general Preferred Applications dialog at the Accessibility tab (see Figure 7-12), where you can set up a screen reader, a magnifier, and predictive text. Ubuntu offers two types of assistance for people who have difficulty reading the screen; these can also be useful for people with good eyesight. The first and probably the most useful is Orca, which reads the text that appears on your computer screen for you. You can choose to run this application at startup. Before doing so, you must run it from a command line. To do this, press Alt-F2 to open the Run Application box, and type the **orca** command. Doing so opens a command prompt where you can select your default language and configure Orca settings that specify exactly what you want Orca to do. Follow the prompts that are offered when you run Orca, and they'll help set up your system.

Figure 7-12. Select Orca in the Preferred Applications interface to have it launched by default as a screen reader.

After you configure Orca for the first time, you can rerun its configuration. To do so, press Alt-F2 to open the Run Application box, and type the **orca** command. This brings up the window shown in Figure 7 13, where you can select the settings you want to use one by one.

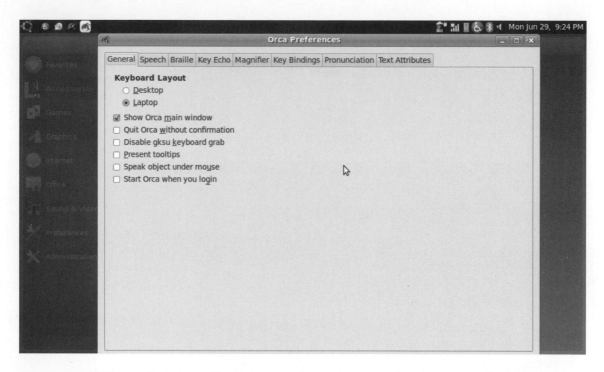

Figure 7-13. To reenter the Orca configuration, run the `orca` *command again to access the Orca Preferences window.*

You have two alternatives to running Orca with its default settings. One is to run Orca with a magnifying glass that you can move over visual elements on your computer screen; the other is to use the GNOME magnifying glass. Both Orca's magnifier and the GNOME magnifier are useful tools; they let you zoom in on what you're doing and make text more readable if changing the resolution isn't sufficient.

The Accessibility tab of the Preferred Applications window also includes a Mobility section. Here you can set up predictive text input via the dasher program. If you want to use this feature, make sure dasher is installed, using Add / Remove programs from the Accessories tab, and select "Run at start" to start the program automatically when you turn on your computer.

Setting Keyboard Accessibility Options

If you need specific features to make working with the keyboard easier, you can find them on the Accessibility tab of the Keyboard Preferences window (see Figure 7-14).

Figure 7-14. If working with the keyboard is hard for you, use the Accessibility features to make it easier.

First is the "Accessibility features can be toggled with keyboard shortcuts" option. Use this option if you want to assign a hot-key sequence to toggle accessibility features on or off; you then use the Layouts options on the Layouts tabs to determine which keys to use for that purpose.

Next are two options related to sticky keys. These options come in handy if you have a problem pressing two keys (like the Alt key and some other key, to access a specific function) simultaneously. By enabling the Sticky Keys feature, you can first press the function key (Shift, Control, Alt, or Fn—anything you would normally use together with another key) and then press the key that provides the function that you need. To switch on this feature, select the "Simulate simultaneous keypresses" option. You may also want to select the option "Disable sticky keys if any two keys are pressed together," which switches off sticky keys easily.

The next two options relate to the speed at which you type. The "Only accept long keypresses" option accepts a keypress only if you press the key for some time. This option can prevent you from accidentally entering text. You may also like the Bounce Keys feature, which ignores a keypress that comes too soon after the previous one. These two options have slide bar you can use to set their associated speed.

Also on the Accessibility tab is the Audio Feedback button. Clicking it displays options that offer audio or visual feedback for keyboard activity, much like the beep you often hear on a cell phone when you press a key. The options in this window speak for themselves (see Figure 7-15).

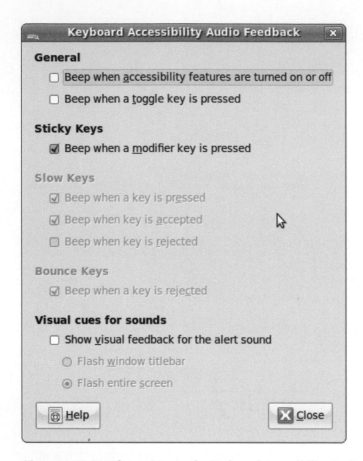

Figure 7-15. Use the options in the Keyboard Accessibility Audio Feedback window for audio/visual support for your keyboard activity.

Selecting Mouse Options for Accessibility

The options on the Mouse Keys tab of the Keyboard Preferences window (see Figure 7-16) aren't as useful. They let you specify that you want to control the mouse pointer using the numeric keypad on your computer. But because most netbooks don't have enough space for a separate numeric keypad, you probably won't use the options offered on this tab.

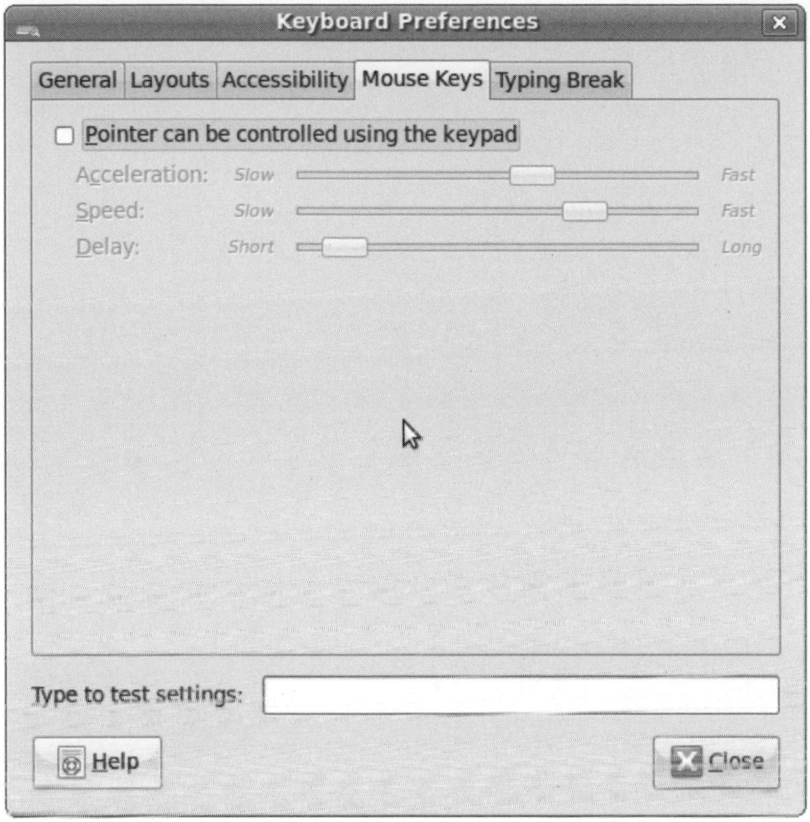

Figure 7-16. On the Mouse Keys tab, you can specify that you want to control the mouse pointer using the numeric keypad on your computer.

Enforcing Regular Breaks

Last but not least, an interesting option helps you prevent injuries related to working on a computer keyboard for too long. This is the option "Lock screen to enforce typing break," which appears on the Typing Break tab of the Keyboard Preferences window (see Figure 7-17). This option helps force you to take a break every so many minutes, during which the screen is locked for a certain amount of time. It's not difficult to use this option: select it, and specify after how much time the break should be activated and how long the break should last. By default, you'll have a 3-minute break every hour. You can cheat if you like, by using the option "Allow postponing of breaks." If you do that, you can postpone a break if you don't want to take it right now.

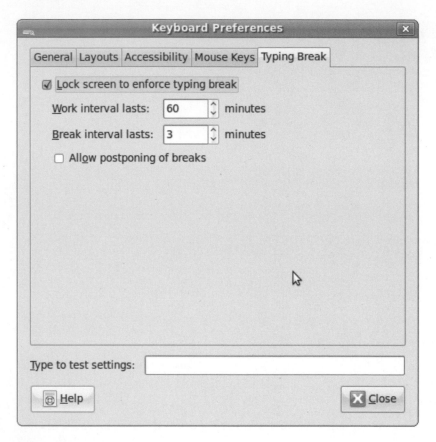

Figure 7-17. To prevent injuries related to working on a keyboard for too long, you can tell your netbook to enforce a regular break.

Changing Display Settings

Last but not least, you can tune your computer's display efficiency. To do so, use the Display icon on the Preferences menu. The options offered (see Figure 7-18) let you select the monitor and resolution you're using. Normally, the default settings are all right; but you can change some options if the installation program didn't detect them correctly. Among these are all normal display-related options, such as the resolution and refresh rate on your computer. Because the installer normally detects the settings of your display as needed, this functionality comes in handy especially when you're using an external monitor.

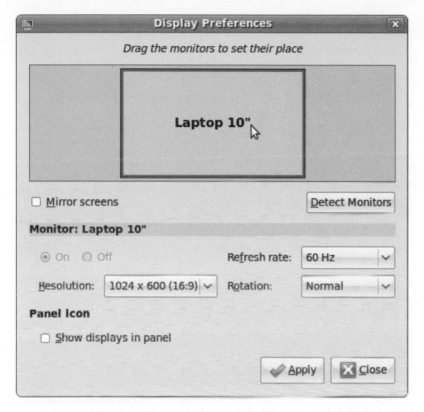

Figure 7-18. The Display Preferences window helps you set useful and less useful options for your display adapter.

Some of the options aren't used as often. Among these is the Detect Monitors button. This is a very useful option that lets you connect to an external monitor, such as a projector that is connected to your computer. Be sure the external monitor is switched on, and then click Detect Monitors. Doing so adds the new monitor to the overview immediately (see Figure 7-19). After the new monitor is detected successfully, you must log off and on again to apply the new settings.

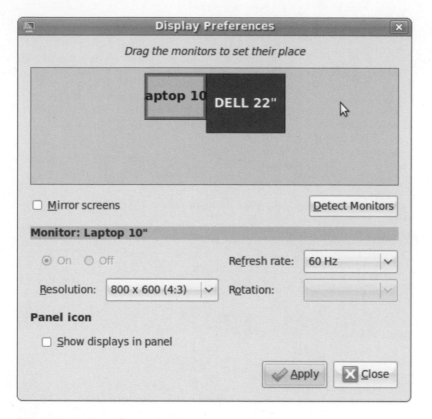

Figure 7-19. To make connecting to an external monitor easy, use the Detect Monitors button.

After you add an external monitor, the configuration program may tell you that it has to set the virtual resolution for you. It proposes to do that automatically, which is a good idea; click Yes.

Another unusual option that is offered from the Display Preferences window is Rotation. It does exactly what it says: it rotates the screen for you. This may be handy if you want to show your display to the person sitting in front of you, or if you want to use your netbook as a DVD-player. (But that is of limited use, because of now no netbook computers have a DVD drive installed.) To use this option, select Normal, Left, Right, or Upside Down from the Rotation drop-down menu. Then, click Apply to apply the setting.

The Display Preferences window also includes the "Mirror screens" option. It lets you run an externally connected monitor or projector as a mirrored desktop or as a separate linked virtual desktop. When you run it as a mirrored desktop, the second display looks exactly the same as the first. When you run is as a separate virtual desktop, the second desktop is independent and functions as an extension of the first desktop. This is useful because it lets you do things like drag a window from one desktop to another. Setting up the vertical position of the two displays isn't hard; simply drag and drop the colored boxes that represent the displays.

Summary

In this chapter, you've learned how to optimize various aspects of your Ubuntu netbook computer. You now know how to tune keyboard and accessibility options. You've also discovered how to modify settings related to power consumption and your display adapter. In the final chapter of this book, you'll learn how to perform administrative tasks on your netbook.

CHAPTER 8

Netbook Management

You've learned how to work with your netbook. Now it's time to examine some management tasks. This chapter teaches you all you need to know to make your netbook do things your way. The following topics are covered:

- Adding and removing software

- Managing the Keyring application

- Managing updates

- Managing users and groups

- An introduction to the command-line interface

Managing Software

Ubuntu Netbook Remix by default comes with lots of useable applications. You may want to change some of the default applications that are installed, remove some of them if you don't like them, or add new applications.

In addition, you can perform management tasks related to working with applications. You need to manage application repositories, which indicate to your computer where it should look for new software. You also need to install updates from time to time. In this section, you'll learn how to do all this.

Installing and Removing Software Packages

Occasionally, you may want to install new software programs on your computer. Ubuntu Netbook Remix has different options that help you do so. The first and easiest is the Add/Remove option on the Accessories tab. When you click this icon, the window shown in Figure 8-1 opens.

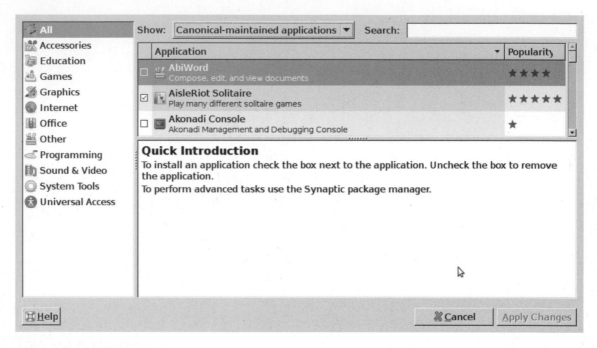

Figure 8-1. *After opening the Add/Remove window, you can see available software.*

The first part to explore is the Show drop-down list in the middle of the upper part of the window. By default, you see only applications that are maintained by Canonical. (Canonical is the company behind Ubuntu.) By selecting Canonical-maintained applications only, you make sure the applications you select will work as you expect on your Ubuntu netbook.

Not all available applications are supported by Canonical. To supplement the Canonical-supported range of software, an additional selection of software—approximately ten times as much—is available for you to use and install, thanks to the wider Ubuntu and free/open source software community. To access this extra software, select "All available applications" from the Show drop-down list. Because the resulting list includes applications that are without support, it gives you more choices but also increases the chance that an application you try to work with will fail.

When you've selected a range of applications to view, you can browse the application categories at left. By default, the list shows all applications. If you want to install an application from a specific category, select the category first. For instance, select Games to see a list of all available games in the Application list in the middle of the screen. While browsing through this list, you'll see a popularity rating and a description for each item (see Figure 8-2).

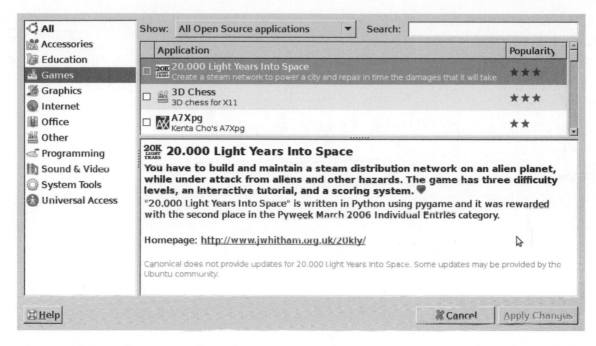

Figure 8-2. *The application installer shows a description and a popularity rating for each of the available applications.*

To install an application, double-click its name or select the check box to the left of the application icon. Depending on what you've selected in the Show drop-down menu, you may get see a pop-up warning you that you're about to install community-enabled software (see Figure 8-3). Click Enable to continue installing the application.

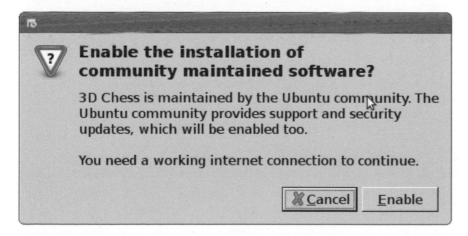

Figure 8-3. *If you're installing a nonsupported application, you may get a warning.*

After you mark an application for installation, you return to the main interface. You can continue marking other applications for installation. Also note that if you want to uninstall an application, you can select "Display installed applications only" from the Show drop-down list, and then uncheck any application you want to uninstall to mark it for removal.

When you're finished marking and unmarking applications, click Apply Changes at lower right. You'll see a pop-up with an overview of all your current selections (see Figure 8-4). If this is what you want to do, click Apply to begin installing and uninstalling.

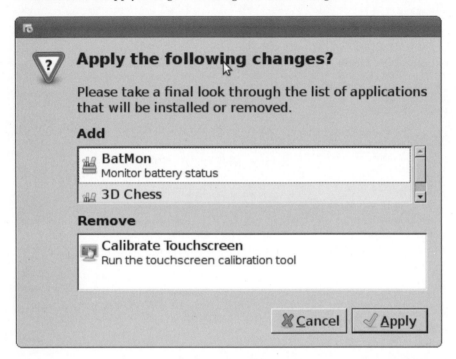

Figure 8-4. Before it begins installing and uninstalling, your computer provides an overview of what it's about to do.

Because installing and removing applications are tasks that require administrator permissions, you must enter your password to confirm that you want to proceed. Then, your newly selected applications are installed on your computer.

■ **Note** I have encountered errors with installation of applications on several occasions. These issues were due to an error in the package-configuration database. If you get errors while installing or updating applications, you can fix it from the command-line interface. From the Accessories tab, open Terminal. Type the command `sudo dpkg --configure -a`. This should repair the errors you're encountering.

Managing Software Repositories

The knowledge of which software you can install comes from software repositories because they let the computer know which software is available. You saw a repository in Chapter 6, in the section "Installing Media Support Using the Medibuntu Repositories." Software repositories are a key component in working with Ubuntu, and they're the reason why software management works completely different in Ubuntu as compared to in Windows or on a Mac. In Windows or on a Mac, if you want to install software, you go to the website of the software developer or vendor, download the software, and install it. After installation, it's hard, if not impossible, for the operating system to keep track of modifications to the installed software.

Ubuntu works with repositories. A *repository* basically is an installation source for software. You teach Ubuntu which repositories it has; and based on these repositories, it creates an index. This index is used to install, manage, and remove software programs. The major benefit is that your operating system is capable of handling updates, with the result that you can work with a more stable computer.

Ubuntu Netbook Remix is configured with a list of default software repositories. These default repositories let you download the most common software packages. The software repository system is great for finding and installing new applications easily, but it really shines when it comes to keeping your installed software up to date. The software installer can check the repositories to find out whether new versions of installed software are available. For that reason, you should always try to install software from repositories only and use no other methods for software installation.

To manage software repositories, you use the Software Sources option from the Administration tab (see Figure 8-5). In this window, you can specify exactly what sources you want to use. First, the Ubuntu Software tab lists which sources are used to install Ubuntu packages. Leave the CD-ROM section unchecked; it's useful only when you have a poor or non-existent internet connection—and in any case, netbooks typically don't have optical drives. A server near your location is selected automatically for installing software packages. The default options on the Ubuntu Software tab are good as they are. Don't change them unless you have particular ethical or legal concerns about some of the restricted software.

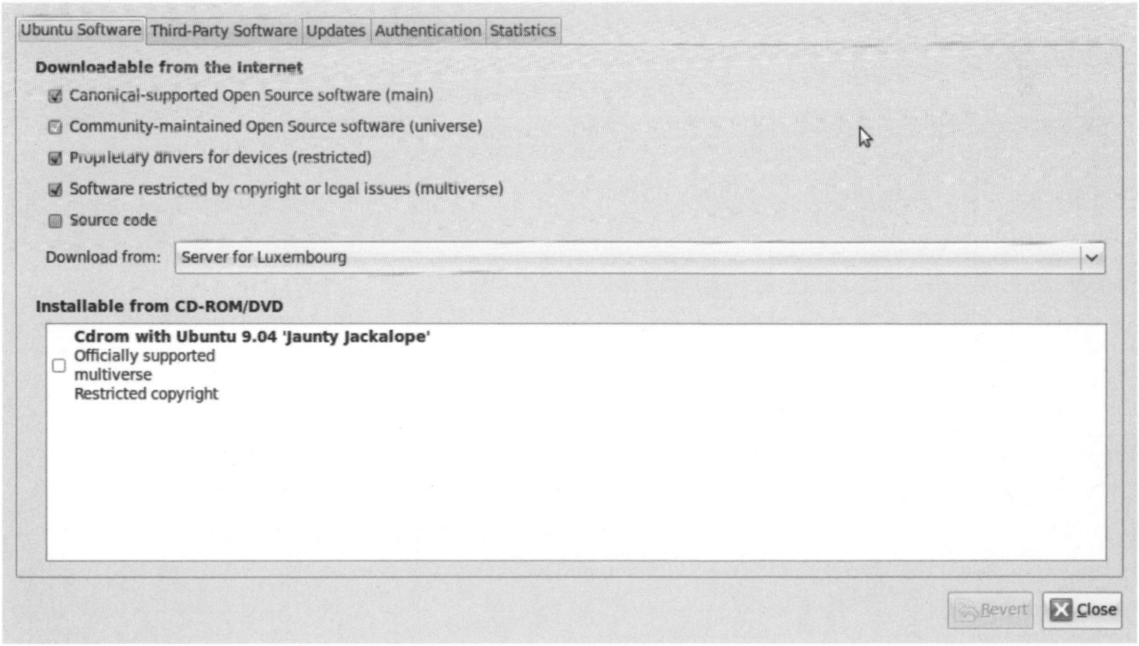

Figure 8-5. You can specify yourself what sources you want to use.

The Third-Party Software tab (see Figure 8-6) lists URLs for software repositories that aren't in the default Ubuntu repositories. An example is the Medibuntu packages, which you learned about in Chapter 6. If you want to include other nondefault packages in your distribution, this is the window where you add them. The following procedure describes how to do that:

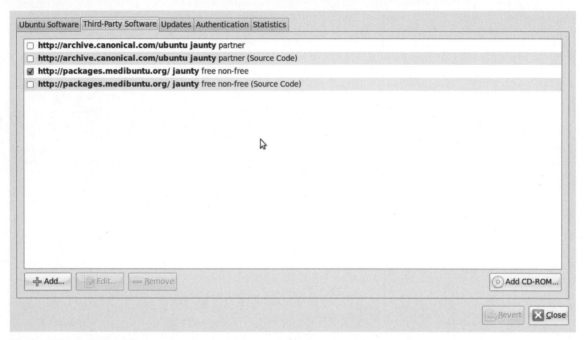

Figure 8-6. *In this window, you can add sources for third-party software packages.*

1. Select the Third-Party Software tab in the Software Sources tool.

2. Click Add to open the window shown in Figure 8-7. This window wants you to add an APT line.

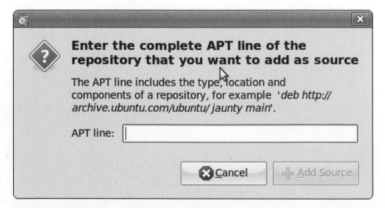

Figure 8-7. *In this window, enter the exact URL you want to use to install a third-party software package.*

3. The installer asks you to enter the installation URL to use, including the type of repository. Make sure you enter the exact URL, including the installation directory, and click Add Source. (For instance, in Chapter 6, you added software from the Medibuntu repositories after adding http://packages.medibuntu.org/jaunty.) This adds the new repository to the list of installation sources and the packages from that repository to the list of available packages.

When you're working with software packages, it's important to be sure you're installing software from a repository that you can trust. To guarantee this, you can import an authentication key. Such a key is normally provided on the site from which you're installing a software package. Make sure the key you want to add is downloaded to the file system of your computer before you add the key with the Software Sources tool.

To add a new key, from the Software Sources tool, open the Authentication tab. It shows a list of trusted software providers you've used before (see Figure 8-8). Click Import Key File to import a new key.

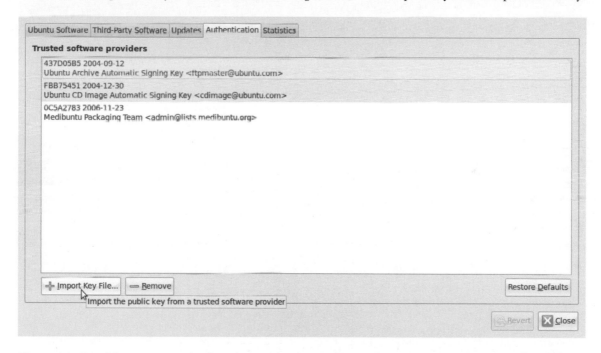

Figure 8-8. *To add a new trusted software provider, use the Import Key File button to import a new key.*

A File Browser window opens, in which you can navigate to the directory where the key file is stored (see Figure 8-9). Select the key file, and click OK to import it. You've now added the new trusted installation source.

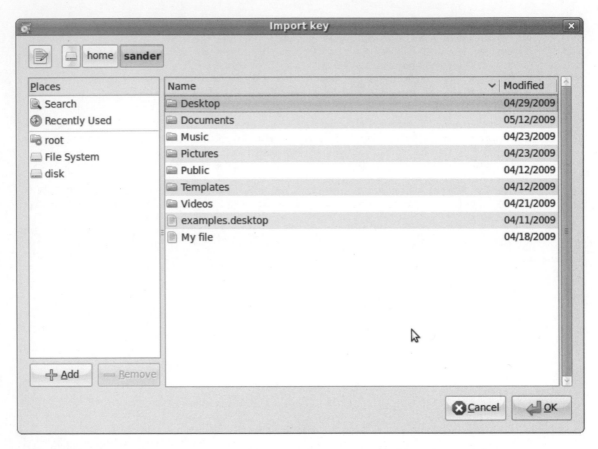

Figure 8-9. Browse to the location containing the key file you want to add, and next click OK to import it.

The last tab in the Software Sources tool is used by Canonical for statistics gathering. Using this option, your computer sends Canonical a list of all software packages you're using. Based on this list, other users can see how popular certain software packages are; and based on that statistical information, other users can more easily determine what to install. Because the information sent is completely anonymous, your privacy isn't at stake; so, if you want to help making Ubuntu even better by participating, click the "Submit statistical information" option on the Statistics tab (see Figure 8-10). If you don't want to do so, no worries—by default, no information is shared with others.

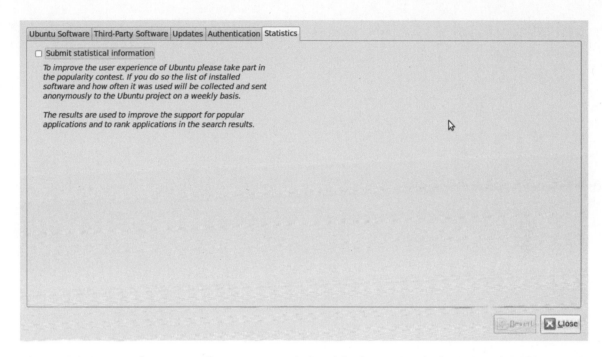

Figure 8-10. You can share your software usage statistics with others using the Statistics tab in the Software Sources program.

Updating Software Packages

Software development on Ubuntu Linux moves quickly. Security updates are released on a regular basis, as are bug fixes. Hence, it's important to make sure your computer is as up to date as it can possibly be. By default, Ubuntu is configured to check for updates and alert you when they're available. But if you'd like to learn more about your setup and make changes to suit your needs, you can configure update management. You first configure the Updates tab in the Software Sources tool; then, you can use the Update Manager to install the updates.

When you select the Updates tab, you see the window shown in Figure 8-11. Various options are available:

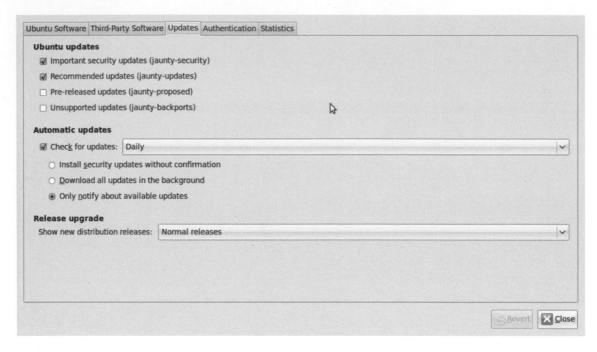

Figure 8-11. This tab specifies how the system handles updates.

- *Important security updates:* This option, which is enabled by default, makes sure security updates are proposed automatically. This is good practice, so don't switch it off.

- *Recommended updates:* If an update is released that fixes a problem, and it has been checked by Canonical, the company will flag it as a recommended update. Recommended updates are also proposed by default, which is good practice, so keep it that way.

- *Pre-released updates:* If you like to work with the most recent versions of software packages, you can select this category. Be aware that using this category may be risky, because prereleased updates aren't necessarily stable. Don't use this option unless you have a good reason.

- *Unsupported updates:* Whereas a prereleased update is waiting for authorization by Canonical, an unsupported update never gets that authorization. Nevertheless, if you're using unsupported packages, you may need these updates. Thus I recommend selecting this option.

- *Check for updates:* By default, your computer checks for updates daily. This is good practice, because it ensures that you're as up to date as possible. But if Internet bandwidth is limited in your geographical region, it may be a good idea to check updates less frequently. If that's the case, select any of the other options that are available: every two days, weekly, or every two weeks.

- *Automatic Updates:* You can specify what to do with automatic updates. By default, the update-management tool only shows a list of available updates—you have to click OK to begin downloading them. If that's too much work, you can choose to download all updates in the background automatically, and even install security updates without confirmation, which may be a good idea if you don't have bandwidth issues.

- *Release upgrade:* You get an automatic notification if a new version of Ubuntu Linux becomes available. The alternatives are to never show this information or to do it only for Long Term Support (LTS) releases. In most cases, the default option (which gives this information for all new normal releases) works fine.

■ **Note** Normally, a new release of Ubuntu Linux is made available every six months. Normal releases are supported for 18 months. Every two years, an LTS version of Ubuntu Linux is released. An LTS release is supported for no less than three years. Thus for a period of three years, you can continue using this version of Ubuntu Linux and know that security updates will be provided, which is ideal for enterprise environments. For most end users, however, there will be no reason not to upgrade to a new release regularly. If you run Ubuntu Netbook Remix on a private computer, you may as well update with every new release.

If you've made changes to the setup for updates, then when you close Software Sources a pop-up will inform you that the information about available software is out of date and will give you the choice to Reload or Close. If you're connected to the Internet, choose Reload. Doing so will synchronize your netbook's software index with the remote servers; if updates are found, the Update Manager will start, and you'll be asked whether you want to install the updates. It's a good idea to do so.

Working with the Update Manager

The Update Manager is an important tool for managing software updates. It checks automatically from time to time to see if specific updates are available; if they are, it opens a window like the one shown in Figure 8-12. In addition, any time you like, you can launch the Update Manager from the Administration tab. It will check for all available updates and present a list, so you can select the packages you want to update.

Figure 8-12. The Update Manager lists all available updates.

If you want to learn more about the software package you're about to install, select the package in question and click the "Description of update" option. Two tabs open in the lower part of the window, and you can read about what has changed compared to the earlier version (see Figure 8-13). This option is useful if you're afraid that the update will break current functionality.

Figure 8-13. If you want to know more about an update before installing it, click the "Description of update" option.

After you select the updates you want to install, click the Install Updates button. You'll be asked for your password, and then the updates will be downloaded (which may take some time) and installed. Before doing so, it makes sense to click the Check button. Doing so ensures that you have all the latest updates.

The Update Manager has some options. You can access these by clicking the Settings button at lower left, which opens the Software Sources tool described earlier to the Updates tab. where, you can select the categories of software that the Update Manager should check for, and how often it should do this (see Figure 8-11 in the previous section).

Managing the Keyring

Probably the most misunderstood component in Ubuntu is the Keyring application. The purpose of the keyring is to manage your passwords and keys. Many applications require the use of a password or some other form of authentication. As a result, the user has to remember too many passwords, and they risk losing access because they can't remember the right password. The keyring offers a solution for this problem.

The idea is simple: the keyring stores all your passwords and encryption keys. When you start your computer, the first application that needs to use one of these passwords or encryption keys prompts you for the keyring's master password. When you enter this master password, all applications that have stored information in the keyring are authorized—you'll never need to enter a password again, as long as you stay in your current session.

Currently, the keyring stores primarily wireless keys and passwords for network shares. Unfortunately, the place you use passwords most often—your browser—isn't supported by the keyring.

The good thing about keyring management is that probably you'll never have to worry about it. Most people never go into the Keyring Manager but are served by the simple initial prompt to set up a master password.

To manage access to the keyring, open the Passwords and Encryption Keys option on the Accessories tab. When an application needs authentication, it will ask you to enter the required credentials. For instance, when you try to connect to a wireless network, the wireless network prompts you for the corresponding WEP or WPA key. If this is the first time you're working with the keyring, you're prompted for a password that will be used as the master password (see Figure 8-14); you can use it to unlock all other passwords that are managed by the keyring.

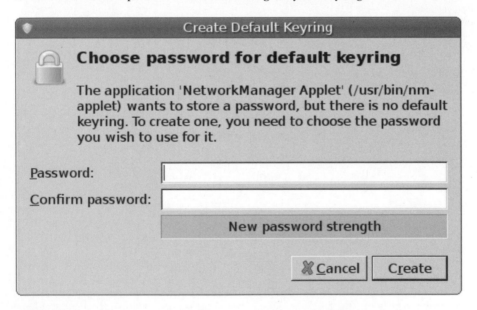

Figure 8-14. When first used, the Keyring application prompts for a password.

While you're entering the password, the keyring shows you how strong it is. Make sure the "New password strength" indicator is as far to the right as possible by entering a password that is at least eight characters long and that includes some punctuation characters and uppercase letters. Then, click Create to set the master password.

■ **Caution** Be sure you use a strong master password. Anyone who gets hold of your laptop and guesses the master password can access all your other passwords.

The next time a new application needs access to a password, it will first prompt you to enter the password (see Figure 8-15). Then, it will automatically add the password to the keyring. If you work with lots of applications that need access to passwords, many passwords will be added to the keyring. The benefit of using the keyring is that the next time you restart your computer, you won't need to enter the password for each individual application—only the master password for the keyring.

Figure 8-15. A new application prompts for a password before adding it to the keyring.

In some cases, you may need to set individual passwords that are managed by the Keyring application and make other changes (normally, you won't need to do so). To do this, open the Accessories tab and select Passwords and Encryption Keys. This window lists all the keys and passwords you've entered (see Figure 8-16).

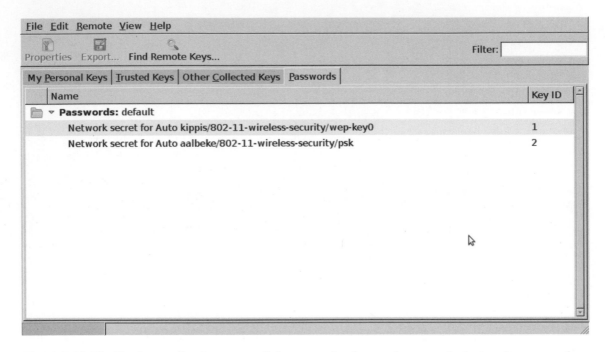

Figure 8-16. *The Keyring application stores all the encryption keys and passwords that you've ever used on your computer.*

Using the Keyring application, you can perform some management tasks on the keys that are stored. Many of the available options are too advanced and you'll never need them. It may however be useful to change the properties of the keys that are stored in the application. To do this, right-click the Keyring folder and choose Unlock. You need to unlock the keyring once—when it's unlocked, the Keyring folder shows a right-pointing arrow that you can click to show the keys the folder contains. To modify their properties, double-click the key or password to open the properties window. It has three tabs (see Figure 8-17) on which the properties of the key or password are stored. You can even see which password is currently stored.

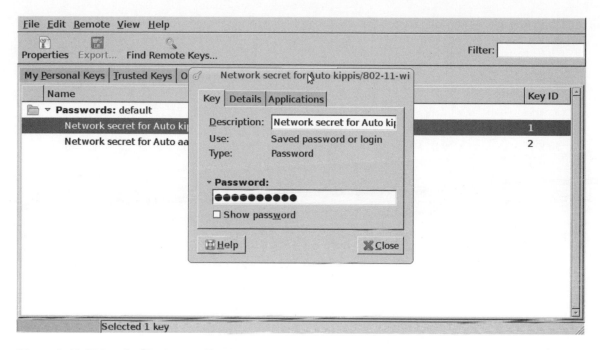

Figure 8-17. Using the Keyring application, you can see the properties of all stored keys and passwords.

When you're trying to access a password for the first time, the Keyring application opens a pop-up, asking if you want to allow access to the Seahorse application (see Figure 8-18). Seahorse is the name for the keyring manager program. From this pop-up, you can specify if you want to allow access once or always.

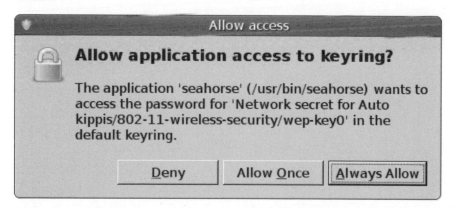

Figure 8-18. Before you can access a password, you need to grant access privileges to the Seahorse application.

When you access the properties of keys and passwords, you can see their technical details (not too interesting in most cases) and, on the Applications tab, which applications have access to the key or password. From this tab, you can also specify the application's access permissions for the key or password (see Figure 8-19). By default, the owning application has all permissions to change or delete the key or password; but if you want to, you can limit the access permissions to make sure a password is protected against accidental removal.

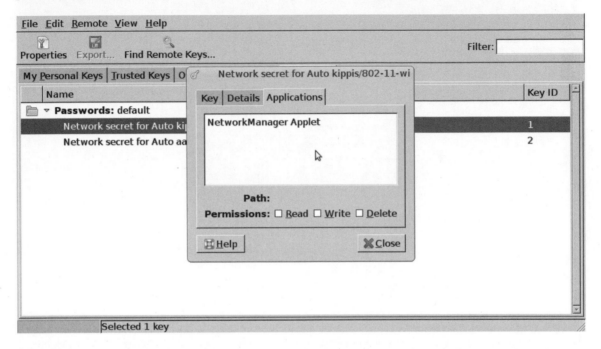

Figure 8-19. For each key or password, you can specify which application has which access permissions.

Another useful management option lets you remove keys or passwords. Using the Keyring application to do this is easy: right-click the key or password you want to remove, and choose Delete from the menu. Doing so removes the key from the keyring. The next time you start the application that used this key, it will prompt you to enter a new key or password, and store that in the keyring.

As a measure of last resort, it's also possible to delete everything currently stored in the keyring. You would need to do this only in extremely rare cases. Doing so basically resets the entire application, allowing you to set it up from scratch the next time an application asks for a key or password. To reset the Keyring application, you must delete its main configuration file. The following procedure shows you how:

1. From the main interface of Ubuntu Netbook Remix, open the File Browser by clicking the home icon.

2. Select View ➤ Show Hidden Files.

3. Open the subdirectory .gnome2 and select keyrings.

4. Select the default.keyring file, and press the Delete key to remove it.

Managing Users and Groups

Chances are, you'll be the only person using your netbook. If you have to share your computer with other people, it's a good idea to create user accounts for them. Group management isn't a common task on Ubuntu Netbook Remix, but occasionally you may need to create a new group to make sure an application can do its work. This section provides a short introduction to user and group management.

To manage users and groups, you use the Users and Groups application in the Administration tab (see Figure 8-20). By default, you have read-only access to this window; to enter management mode, click Unlock and enter your password.

Figure 8-20. To get full access to the user and group management tool, you need to unlock it first.

In management mode, you can add new users and groups, delete existing users and groups, and change the properties of current users and groups. The following procedure explains how to create a new user. It also discusses the relevant properties you can set for users:

1. To create a new user, click the Add User button. Doing so opens the Account tab in the "New user account" window (see Figure 8-21). On this tab, enter a username followed by the user's real name.

Figure 8-21. On the Account tab, you enter the settings you want to use for the new user account.

2. Specify a profile for the user. You can choose from three profiles: an Unprivileged user, a Desktop user, or an Administrator. By default, new users are created as Desktop users. This gives the user a home directory where they can store personal files and allows the user to launch applications but not change things. If you want to give your user full access, select the Administrator profile; or select Unprivileged user to minimize the user's options. (You probably won't want to make your new user Unprivileged, because that prevents them from accessing the network, listening to music, and using their USB flash drive, among other things.)

3. As the last essential component, the user must have a password. Enter the password yourself, or use the "Generate random password" option if you aren't creative enough to come up with a good password.

4. On the Contact tab in the "New user account" window (see Figure 8-22), enter contact details for the user. These include the user's office location, work phone number, and home phone number. You aren't required to enter this information; it's optional.

Figure 8-22. To make identifying a user easier, you can enter an office location and phone numbers.

5   On the User Privileges tab, specify what you want to allow the new user to do
     (see Figure 8-23). Based on the profile you selected for the new user in step 2,
     these user privileges have been set automatically, but you may want to make
     some changes. For an administrator, select all the options. For normal desktop
     users, I recommend changing the default selection to include at least the
     following:

     •   Access external storage devices automatically: Lets the user access files on
         external media, such as USB drives and other flash media

     •   Connect to wireless and ethernet networks: Lets the user connect to the
         Internet

     •   Use audio devices: Lets the user use a microphone and listen to audio files or
         streaming media with the netbook

     •   Configure printers: Lets the user set up a new printer when connecting to a
         printer at a new location

The other options aren't required for most ordinary users, although you may find some exceptions in specific situations.

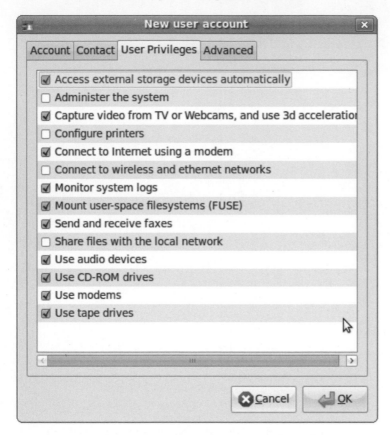

Figure 8-23. You may want to apply some changes to the default user privileges that are granted.

6.   On the last tab of the "New user account" window, you'll find some advanced options (see Figure 8-24). Handling these is easy: accept the default settings. If you're an experienced Linux user or administrator, you may need to change some items here (and in that case, you'll know exactly what you need to change). In all other cases, the defaults work fine.

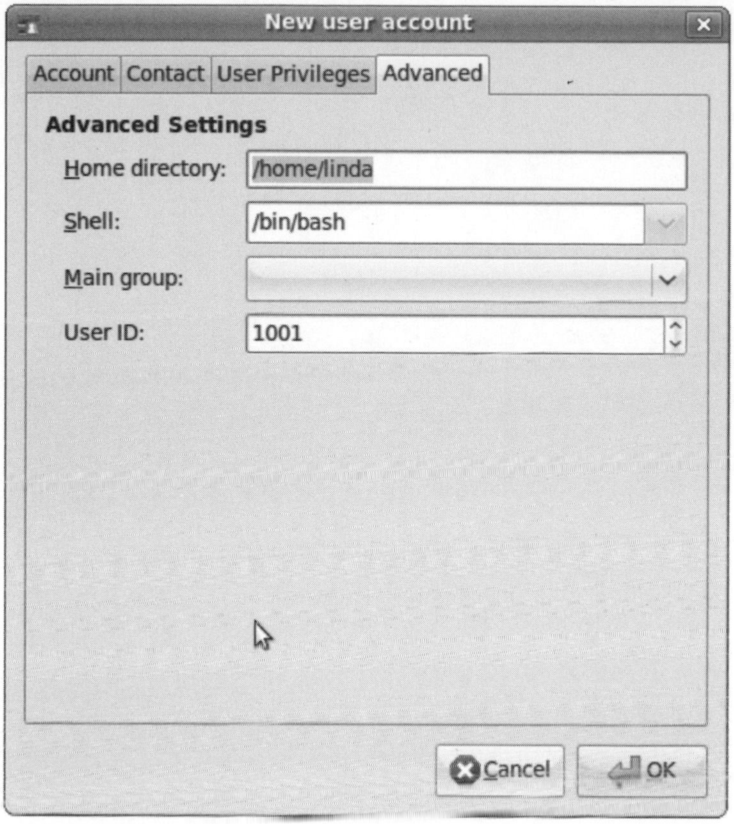

Figure 8-24. In almost all cases, you can accept the default selections on the Advanced tab.

In rare cases, you'll need to configure new group accounts. You may want to create a group if you need to give access to certain files to specific users only. On a personal netbook, however, this won't happen often. To create a new group, in the main window of the Users and Groups tool, click Manage Groups. The resulting window lists all existing groups (see Figure 8-25). Click Add Group to add a new group.

Figure 8-25. In the Groups settings window, click Add Group to add a new group.

When you create a new group, you must specify three things (see Figure 8-26). First, you enter the name of the new group. Pick whatever you want, as long as it makes sense to you. Next, you need a group ID. Every Linux group has a unique numeric ID; it's generated automatically for you, and you can safely accept the default ID that is created. Last, specify which users are members of the group. There is no need to include the root user. *Root* is the almighty system administrator on your computer: they can access all files and services already. For the rest, include all users whom you want to give permissions via this group.

Figure 8-26. To create a new group, enter a name for the group and specify its members.

Using a Printer

Adding a printer on Ubuntu is easy in most situations. Connect the printer's USB cable to your netbook computer, and the netbook will automatically do everything that is needed to install the printer. Give your computer a minute, and it will show you the new printer (see Figure 8-27).

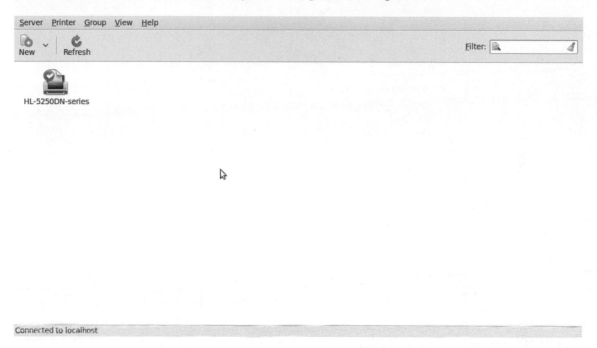

Figure 8-27. After you attach a new printer, your computer automatically configures it.

If, after installing the printer, you need to change some of its parameters, open the Printing program from the Administration tab, and double-click the printer whose properties you want to change. In the Printer Properties window that opens (see Figure 8-28), you can change most of the printer's settings.

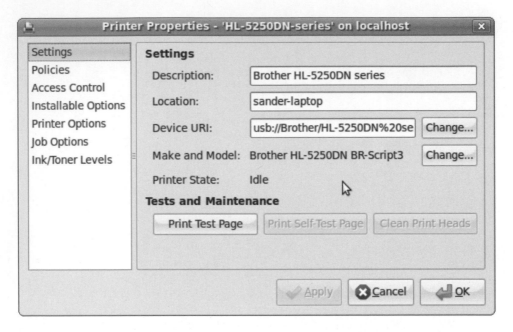

Figure 8-28. In the Printer Properties window, you can change the properties of existing printers.

Printer properties are listed in seven categories. By default, you see the Settings options, which include the name of your computer and printer. Normally, these options are for informational purposes only. The most useable option here is Print Test Page, which lets you check whether your printer can print a test page properly.

To determine what your printer can and can't do, you can use policies. The Policies options (see Figure 8-29) show the current status of your printer. By default, the state of your printer is fully operational: the options Enabled, Accepting jobs, and Shared are selected. Next, the Error Policy states that when a print job can't be printed, it should be offered to the printer again. Operation Policy doesn't give you any choice other than the default option, "Default behavior." Last, you can specify whether your printer should use a starting banner and an ending banner. A *banner* is a piece of paper printed before and/or after each print job, which makes it easier to identify a print job on a printer used by many people. In general, banners are a waste of paper.

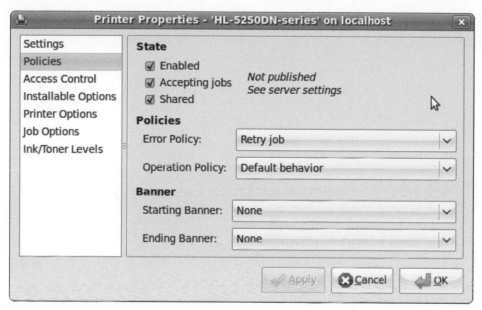

Figure 8-29. Policies options let you define how your printer should be used.

The Access Control options (see Figure 8-30) let you make lists of users and allow or deny them access to your printer. This is useful in corporate environments where many people can access many printers, but the typical netbook user doesn't need these options.

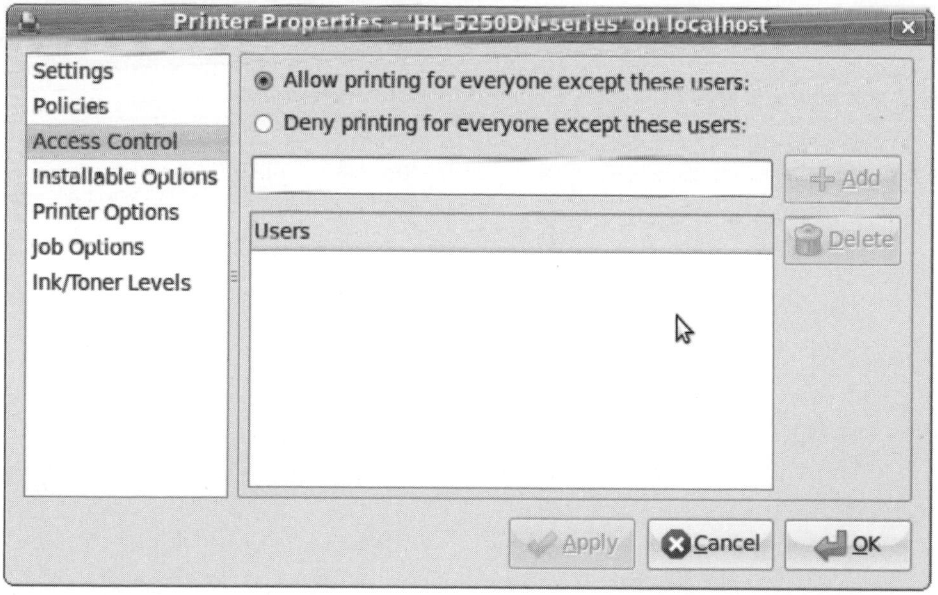

Figure 8-30. Access Control lets you allow or deny access to your printer for specific users.

■ **Note** Depending on the type of printer, you may or may not see some of the tabs discussed here.

Some printers also offer options on other tabs. On these tabs, you'll find options specific for that printer. For instance, on my printer you can see the input trays only as printer-specific options, whereas other printers may show (many) other options.

One of the more important printer property pages is Printer Options (see Figure 8-31). These options are related to the type of paper and the print quality you're using. The following options are available:

- *Media Size:* This option defines the type of paper you're using. The default setting is Letter. Check that this is the correct paper size for your region/printer. In Europe, for instance, you may have to change this to A4 paper (although this should have been set automatically when you set your location while installing the operating system).

- *Print Quality:* The default 600 dpi print quality used on the printer in this example gives nice quality printouts. If you're printing a document so you can do a text revision on the morning train, you don't need the highest quality. In that case, select a lower print quality, to avoid using as much ink.

- *Media Type:* By default, the media type is set to Plain Paper, but there are lots of other options. Using this option, you can instruct your printer to print envelopes, slides, or other types of media.

- *Manual Feed:* Select this option if you want to insert the media to be used one by one.

- *Duplex:* To print on both sides of your media, specify a duplex setting. Use No Tumble to have the top of the page the same on both sides of the media; use Tumble to print the other side upside down.

- *Toner Save:* Switch on this option to save the maximum amount of toner.

- *Sleep Time:* Use this setting to define when the printer should be switched from standby mode to off.

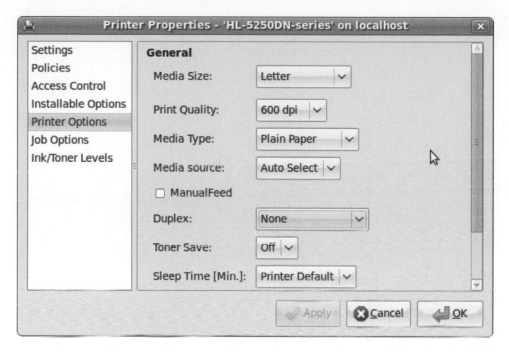

Figure 8-31. *On the Printer Options tab, you find some important options related to the quality of your prints.*

Following the printer options is the Job Options tab (see Figure 8-32). Here, you can define how a print job is printed. Among others options, you can define how many copies to print and what orientation (landscape or portrait) to use. You can also instruct the printer to scale the print job so it fits on the page, or to print several pages per side. Text options let you set margins for your print job; however, you generally access these from the program you use to create the document (more on such applications is in Chapter 5).

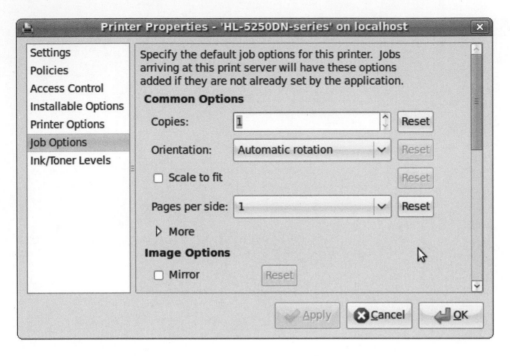

Figure 8-32. The Job Options tab has useful options, such as the number of copies you want to print.

Last, if your printer supports it, is the Ink/Toner Levels tab. To use it, your printer must support software that reads the current toner level. If your printer doesn't, you'll see that your printer lacks support for these options.

Adding a Network Printer

Instead of working with local printers, you can add network printers to your netbook. To do this, in the Add Printer dialog, click the New button. Then, in the Select Device window, click the triangle next to Network Printer to access all available options to add a network printer (see Figure 8-33).

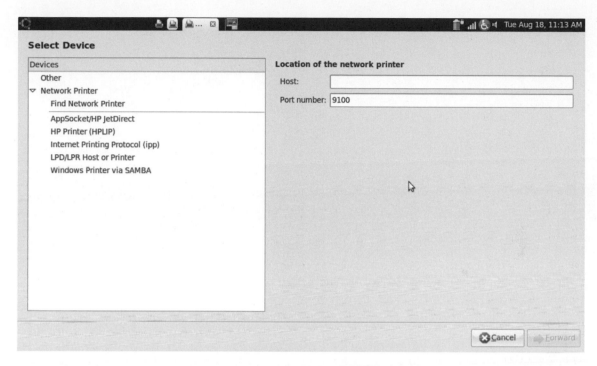

Figure 8-33. Ubuntu gives you options to add different kind of network printers.

In this window, you first need to specify what type of network printer you're using. It's not a bad idea to try the Find Network Printer option first, which helps you find a printer by the name of the host it's connected to.

If that doesn't work, you'll need the Windows Printer via SAMBA option in most cases. This option assumes you have a printer that is attached to a Windows computer somewhere in your network and which you've shared on that computer. Enter the name of the computer followed by the name of the printer (see Figure 8-34), and click Forward. Your netbook will connect with the printer and automatically install the drivers it needs. If it can't determine which drivers these are, a pop-up opens in which you can select your printer make and model. Then, click Forward to complete installation of the network printer. You can now print documents to that printer.

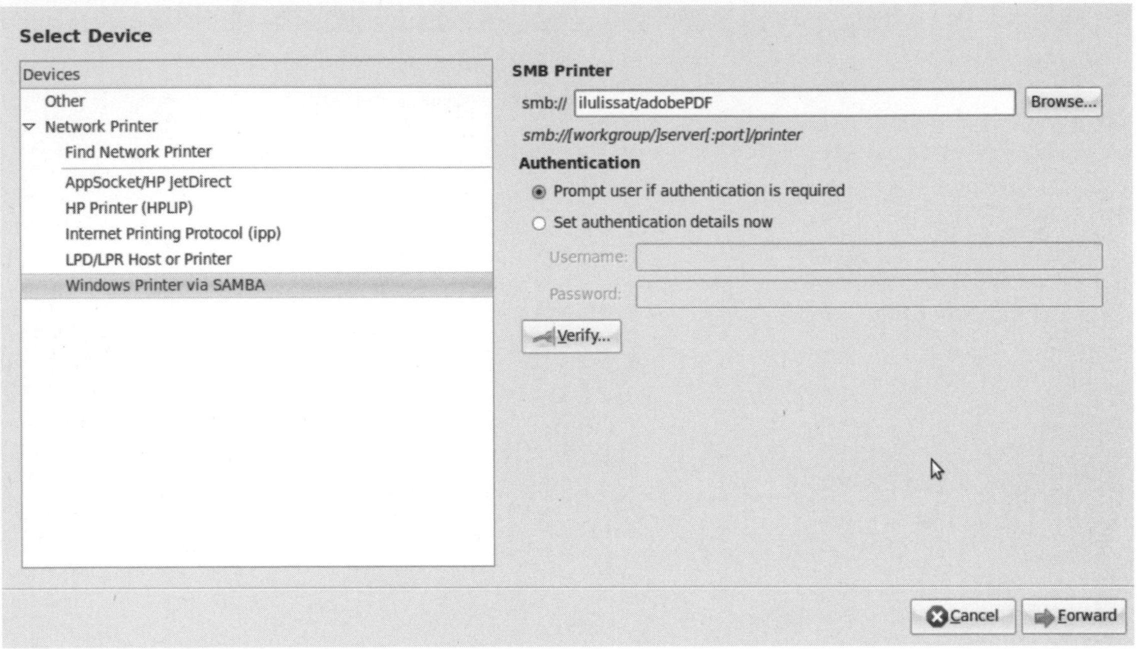

Figure 8-34. Specify the protocol and address to print to your network printer.

An Introduction to Working on the Command-Line Interface

In most situations, you can perform the tasks you need by using one of the graphical applications offered by Ubuntu Netbook Remix. But in some cases, the graphical applications aren't sufficient, and you need to access the command-line interface. For instance, the graphical interface gives you no way to terminate all processes that have *http* in their name or path; but you can do this easily from the command line with a command such as kill `ps aux | grep http | awk '{ print $2 }`'. As you can imagine, though, you need some training before you can use commands like this.

You should build up your skill by starting with simple commands such as ls, which shows a list of files in the current directory; or ping, which lets you test whether you can reach another computer on the Internet.

To access the command-line interface, click the Terminal icon on the Accessories tab. Doing so opens the window shown in Figure 8-35.

■ **Note** In the Ubuntu forums, you'll often see commands used as solutions to problems. Working with these isn't hard: you can copy them from your browser window and paste them on the command-line interface. This technique is simple, and there's almost no risk of making typing errors. But be aware of what you're doing— copying random commands that you find on the Internet can be dangerous!

```
File  Edit  View  Terminal  Help
sander@sander-laptop:~$
```

Figure 8-35. *For more avanced management tasks, Ubuntu Netbook Remix offers the command-line interface from the Terminal.*

Managing a Linux computer from the command-line interface is a completely different subject, which merits a book of its own. Linux offers many commands that let skilled users perform advanced configuration and management tasks. Knowledge of these tasks is especially useful if you're planning to get involved with Linux server management. If you want to become skilled on the Linux command line, I recommend my book *Beginning the Linux Command Line* (Apress, 2009).

As a normal user, you'll occasionally find directions on the Internet to accomplish certain tasks from the command line. These tasks may involve typing a command or changing a configuration file using an editor.

Entering Commands

When you type commands at the command line, the user account you use is important. By default, after opening the command-line interface, you're logged in as your username. This user account has limited permissions and can't perform all administrative tasks. To unleash the full power of the Linux command line, you must get administrator permissions. The Linux equivalent of being administrator is being root. The user root is the almighty system administrator of a Linux computer and knows no limitations.

To get root permissions, you can use two common methods:

- Use the sudo su command.

- Use sudo in front of each command.

The first method makes you root. From the moment you type sudo su until the moment you close your session using the exit command, you have full permissions on your computer. This is convenient

233

if you're an administrator and know exactly what you're doing. If you aren't, I recommend not using this method. A small error may have big results, which can result in making your computer inaccessible. Also, it's easy to accidentally leave open a Terminal window that's logged in as root and do damage by running something with more permissions than you thought you had. It's best to invoke the root user only when you need it.

Thus the better way to perform a command with root permissions is to add `sudo` in front of the command. For example, instead of `rm /tmp/file`, you type `sudo rm /tmp/file`. Remember that you must use `sudo` in front of *every* command you want to execute with root permissions.

Changing Configuration Files

On Linux, system settings are stored in plain-text configuration files that you can edit to change your configuration. Don't let yourself be driven crazy by experienced Linux administrators, who frequently use hard-to-use editors such as vi to change the configuration files directly. As a Linux user, you can usually find alternatives to the text configuration files in a graphical program. For those few cases where you can't, you can use the Text Editor from the Accessories tab (see Figure 8-36).

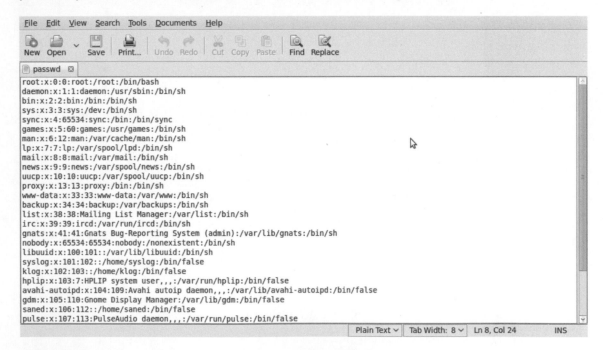

Figure 8-36. In the Text Editor, you can change configuration files.

Be aware that when you use the Text Editor as a normal user, you get the permissions associated with normal users. To change a configuration file, you need root permissions. The best way to get these permissions is to open a terminal window as described in the previous section and type the command `sudo gedit`. This opens the Text Editor in root mode, so you can change any configuration file you like. Alternatively, you can press Alt-F2 to open the Run Application dialog, and typing `gksudo gedit`.

Summary

In this chapter, you've learned about some administrative tasks you may need to perform when using Ubuntu Netbook Remix. First, you learned how to manage applications. Next, you explored how to manage the Keyring application, which manages passwords and encryption keys on your computer. You also read how to create new user accounts and groups, which makes working with others must easier. The next section explained how to configure printers on your computer. In the last part of this chapter, you got a brief introduction to working on the command line.

I hope this book has been helpful to you and that you enjoy working with Ubuntu on your netbook computer!

Index

You Need the Companion eBook

Your purchase of this book entitles you to buy the companion PDF-version eBook for only $10. Take the weightless companion with you anywhere.

We believe this Apress title will prove so indispensable that you'll want to carry it with you everywhere, which is why we are offering the companion eBook (in PDF format) for $10 to customers who purchase this book now. Convenient and fully searchable, the PDF version of any content-rich, page-heavy Apress book makes a valuable addition to your programming library. You can easily find and copy code—or perform examples by quickly toggling between instructions and the application. Even simultaneously tackling a donut, diet soda, and complex code becomes simplified with hands-free eBooks!

Once you purchase your book, getting the $10 companion eBook is simple:

❶ Visit **www.apress.com/promo/tendollars/**.

❷ Complete a basic registration form to receive a randomly generated question about this title.

❸ Answer the question correctly in 60 seconds, and you will receive a promotional code to redeem for the $10.00 eBook.

eBookshop

Apress®
THE EXPERT'S VOICE™

233 Spring Street, New York, NY 10013